DATE DUE

FEB 0 4 2008			
OCT 16 2019			

Demco, Inc. 38-293

A World Upside Down and Backwards

READING AND LEARNING DISORDERS

THE ENCYCLOPEDIA OF PSYCHOLOGICAL DISORDERS

THE ENCYCLOPEDIA OF PSYCHOLOGICAL DISORDERS

Senior Consulting Editor Carol C. Nadelson, M.D.
Consulting Editor Claire E. Reinburg

A World Upside Down and Backwards
READING AND LEARNING DISORDERS

Elizabeth Russell Connelly

CHELSEA HOUSE PUBLISHERS
Philadelphia

The ENCYCLOPEDIA OF PSYCHOLOGICAL DISORDERS provides up-to-date information on the history of, causes and effects of, and treatment and therapies for problems affecting the human mind. The titles in this series are not intended to take the place of the professional advice of a psychiatrist or mental health care professional.

Chelsea House Publishers
Editor in Chief: Stephen Reginald
Managing Editor: James D. Gallagher
Production Manager: Pamela Loos
Art Director: Sara Davis
Director of Photography: Judy L. Hasday
Senior Production Editor: Lisa Chippendale

Staff for A WORLD UPSIDE DOWN AND BACKWARDS
Editorial Assistants: Lily Sprague, Heather Forkos
Picture Researcher: Sandy Jones
Associate Art Director: Takeshi Takahashi
Designer: Brian Wible
Cover Design: Brian Wible

The ChelseaHouse World Wide Web site address is
http://www.chelseahouse.com

First Printing.

9 8 7 6 5 4 3 2 1

Library of Congress Cataloging-in-Publication Data

Connelly, Elizabeth.

A world upside down and backward: reading and other learning disorders / by
Elizabeth Russell Connelly.
    p.cm. — (Encyclopedia of psychological disorders)
Includes bibliographical references (p.) and index.
ISBN 0-7910-4894-2
1. Learning disabilities. 2. Reading disability. I. Title. II. Series.
LC4704.C672 1999
371.91'44—dc21   98-42892
                                                                        CIP

CONTENTS

PSYCHOLOGICAL DISORDERS AND THEIR EFFECT

CAROL C. NADELSON, M.D.
PRESIDENT AND CHIEF EXECUTIVE OFFICER,
The American Psychiatric Press

There are a wide range of problems that are considered psychological disorders, including mental and emotional disorders, problems related to alcohol and drug abuse, and some diseases that cause both emotional and physical symptoms. Psychological disorders often begin in early childhood, but during adolescence we see a sharp increase in the number of people affected by these disorders. It has been estimated that about 20 percent of the U.S. population will have some form of mental disorder sometime during their lifetime. Some psychological disorders appear following severe stress or trauma. Others appear to occur more often in some families and may have a genetic or inherited component. Still other disorders do not seem to be connected to any cause we can yet identify. There has been a great deal of attention paid to learning about the causes and treatments of these disorders, and exciting new research has taught us a great deal in the last few decades.

The fact that many new and successful treatments are available makes it especially important that we reject old prejudices and outmoded ideas that consider mental disorders to be untreatable. If psychological problems are identified early, it is possible to prevent serious consequences. We should not keep these problems hidden or feel shame that we or a member of our family has a mental disorder. Some people believe that something they said or did caused a mental disorder. Some people think that these disorders are "only in your head" so that you could "snap out of it" if you made the effort. This type of thinking implies that a treatment is a matter of willpower or motivation. It is a terrible burden for someone who is suffering to be blamed for their misery, and often people with psychological disorders are not treated compassionately. We hope that the information in this book will teach you about various mental illnesses.

The problems covered in the volumes in the ENCYCLOPEDIA OF PSYCHOLOGICAL DISORDERS were selected because they are of particular importance to young adults, because they affect them directly or because they affect family and friends. There are individual volumes on reading disorders, attention deficit and disruptive behavior disorders, and dementia—all of these are related to our abilities to learn and integrate information from the world around us. There are books on drug abuse that provide useful information about the effects of these drugs and treatments that are available for those individuals who have drug problems. Some of the books concentrate on one of the most common mental disorders, depression. Others deal with eating disorders, which are dangerous illnesses that affect a large number of young adults, especially women.

Most of the public attention paid to these disorders arises from a particular incident involving a celebrity that awakens us to our own vulnerability to psychological problems. These incidents of celebrities or public figures revealing their own psychological problems can also enable us to think about what we can do to prevent and treat these types of problems.

OVERVIEW: LEARNING DISORDERS

Learning disorders are lifelong conditions that can affect much of a person's life, including daily routines, family relationships, schoolwork, and even friendships. Although some people may have a single, isolated learning problem that has little impact on other areas of their lives, others experience many overlapping learning disabilities that cause difficulties in all areas (Neuwirth, 1993).

Unlike many other disabilities, such as paralysis or blindness, a learning disorder is hidden. A learning disorder does not disfigure someone or leave other visible signs that might invite others to offer understanding or support. Learning disorders affect people's ability to link information from different parts of the brain and to interpret what they see and hear. These limitations can show up in many ways— as specific difficulties with spoken and written language, coordination, self-control, or attention. Such difficulties extend to schoolwork and can interfere with learning to read, write, or do math (Neuwirth, 1993).

What are reading and learning disorders? Most of us have probably heard of the most common learning disorder—dyslexia, or reading disorder. But there are also mathematics disorders and disorders of written expression.

Rarely do any of the three types occur alone; more often, they overlap. Those who have heard of dyslexia most likely think of a friend or classmate who reverses certain letters or speaks slowly. But in more extreme cases, children with dyslexia appear to have severe problems with the simplest rules of language. For example, they may struggle over words such as "it" and "the," have trouble distinguishing between "from" and "form," or be unable to decipher the question when asked to name a word that rhymes with "bat." Unfortunately, children with learning disorders are often labeled "dumb" by their classmates, whereas, in fact, their intelligence level is usually the same as, if not higher than, that of their peers.

The cause of dyslexia is unknown; however, it is believed to be a combination of physiological, neurological, and genetic factors. Some studies indicate that a learning disorder can result from the failure of one side of the brain to gain dominance over the other side. The disorder involves impairment in one or more of the basic psychological processes of understanding or using language, usually revealed by an imperfect ability to listen, think, speak, read, write, spell, or do mathematical calculations. The term "learning disorder" is not applicable to children who have learning problems caused mainly by impairment of vision or hearing, or by physical disabilities, mental retardation, or emotional disturbance. Nor is it termed a learning disorder when a student has a cultural or economic disadvantage, or if he or she has received inadequate instruction.

According to the American Psychiatric Association (APA), learning disorders are usually first diagnosed in childhood or early adolescence. The three major types—reading disorder, mathematics disorder, and disorder of written expression—with others, comprise the broad subclass of specific developmental disorders. For many people with these disorders, early diagnosis can increase the likelihood for more productive lives, but there is no known cure for learning disorders. An individual's success depends on the degree to which he or she learns to compensate for his or her disability.

In this volume of ENCYCLOPEDIA OF PSYCHOLOGICAL DISORDERS, we attempt to answer the most fundamental questions about learning disorders. Chapter 1 provides an overview, highlighting the features of reading, mathematics, and writing disorders. To help readers understand how those with learning disorders can achieve great success, a case study describes some of the real-life difficulties faced by one of history's great military leaders. In Chapter 2, we trace the history of learning disorders, touching on the evolution of our understanding of these disorders as well as how our society has responded to the needs of those struggling with these problems.

Many of us may see the signs of learning disorders in brothers and sisters or classmates and peers, but unless we have a learning disorder ourselves, we can't know how they feel. To that end, Chapter 3 examines the criteria for diagnosing these disorders and probes deeper into describing how the disorders and their possible complications can affect the day-to-day lives of learning-disabled individuals. Two case reports provide readers with insight into the struggles faced by real people. In Chapter 4, we look at learning disorders from the broader perspective of society. Chapter 5 steps back a bit to discuss various hypotheses—some well-established and a few yet to be supported—about what causes learning disabilities. Finally, in Chapter 6, we outline a number of methods typically used to treat the emotional stress and behavioral problems associated with these disorders.

A young girl tries to remember how to spell the words on her spelling list. Children with learning disorders may find it hard to associate spoken words with the written-out letters.

1

DEFINING LEARNING DISORDERS

A learning disorder is a neurobiological disorder, meaning that there are differences in brain structure or function that lead to difficulty in learning to read, write expressively, speak, or compute math. These differences impede the ability to store, process, or produce information. People with learning disabilities have trouble learning because their minds process words or information differently than people who learn normally. They are generally of normal or above-average intelligence, but their learning disorder creates a gap between their ability and their performance (Lyon, 1995).

Although learning disorders do not go away, people can learn to work with their areas of difficulty and lead productive, independent lives. The following illustrates how one man with a learning disorder did just that, ultimately emerging as a world-famous military leader of World War II.

■   ■   ■

General George S. Patton Jr. was one of the United States' greatest generals. Considered a genius in tank warfare, Patton, with his superior planning, understanding of modern combat, and judgment, was essential to the Allied victory in World War II. His greatest accomplishment was pushing the U.S. Third Army across France and Germany in 1944–45, forcing a German surrender.

Patton inherited all of the desirable traits of a long line of exceptionally gifted ancestors from both sides of his family, the transmission of the physical attributes from both grandfathers being nothing short of astounding. (When fitted for his uniform at Virginia Military Institute [VMI], for example, he had the same measurements as his father and grandfather before him.) In addition

General George S. Patton Jr., one of the United States' great military leaders, overcame dyslexia to rise to a post of high honor and responsibility in the army.

to having such traits as physical prowess, endurance, ambition, and high intelligence, however, Patton also had a reading disorder.

Young George's dyslexia played a decisive role in shaping his personality in a family with an intense and pervasive preoccupation with family tradition. "The Boy," as he was affectionately known, was not sent to school until he was 11 years old. George's parents realized early on that their son had a developmental reading disorder, although the concept itself was not formally defined at the time. His devoted parents instinctively did the right thing for him by providing an alternative education, using spoken words: they and an ever-present maternal aunt read to George for several hours each day. They also encouraged and supported his talents. When they thought George was ready, they sent him to a supportive private school whose staff was open to providing him with an individualized curriculum.

In spite of getting help and unwavering support and love from his family, Patton suffered serious problems from a lack of self-esteem throughout his life, probably as a result of his dyslexia. However, Patton was motivated to overcome the handicaps of dyslexia in a world that made no allowance for the disorder. Despite his frustration in school, he graduated from both VMI and the United States Military Academy at West Point. He accumulated vast amounts of knowledge throughout his life—first by memorization from being read to and taught by his family, and later by his own systematic and diligent reading of large numbers of books. Patton was easily the best educated and best read American military leader of World War II.

Also critical to Patton's success was the understanding and support of his wife, Beatrice, who encouraged him throughout his military career. Patton's public image was a tough-talking, seemingly willful leader, but those close to him knew him to be a sensitive, affectionate, and caring person. His dyslexia went virtually unnoticed by others (Fras, 1996).

■   ■   ■

General Patton's story reveals how many factors can be instrumental in successfully overcoming a developmental disorder like dyslexia. Patton benefited from supportive and attentive parents, a history of outstanding family role models, perceptive school teachers, and, later, a supportive spouse. Patton's extraordinary achievements would not have been possible without these influences, combind with his own determination to master dyslexia.

Approximately 10 percent of the U.S. population have some form of learning disability. An estimated five percent of the students in public schools in the United States are identified as having a learning disorder. And slightly more than half of all public school students in special education programs have learning disorders.

Walt Disney, creator of Mickey Mouse and the Disney entertainment company, did not let his learning disorder keep him from success. Many people with reading problems are talented in other areas, such as the visual arts.

CLINICAL DESCRIPTION

The APA defines learning disorders as development difficulties that include three groups: reading disorders, mathematics disorders, and written expression disorders. Learning disorders are suspected when the individual's scores on standardized tests in reading, mathematics, or written expression are substantially below the level expected for his or her age, schooling, and intelligence. The learning problems must interfere significantly with the child's academic achievement or daily activities to be considered an actual disorder.

Problems with basic reading skills are the most common and often the most debilitating forms of learning disorders. Difficulties with expressive writing (for example, writing a critical essay) or mathematics skills may also signal a learning disorder. All three disorders can occur with—and be complicated by—problems in attention and the development of social skills. This, in turn, can lead to difficulties in social relationships, such as building friendships.

"Learning disorder not otherwise specified" is a category designated by the American Psychiatric Association (APA) for difficulties in learning that do not meet the APA's criteria for any specific learning disorder. This category might include a young person who has a problem in all three areas (reading, mathematics, and written expression) that, collectively, interferes with academic achievement, even though individually each skill is not too much below the norm. Persons with learning disorders commonly also have problems with communication or a lack of motor skills, and perhaps exhibit other symptoms of anxiety, motivational problems, or associated psychiatric disorders.

Learning disabilities have distinct characteristics and should not be confused with mental retardation, autism, deafness, blindness, or behavioral disorders—none of which is a learning disorder. Learning disorders should also not be confused with academic difficulties that result from lack of opportunity or cultural factors. Students who have had inadequate schooling often perform poorly on standardized achievement tests, and in day-to-day class work they are likely to have problems with spelling and basic language skills. Children from ethnic or cultural backgrounds in which English is not the primary language also may not do as well as English-speaking students. Children from poor backgrounds may be at greater risk for absenteeism due to more frequent illnesses or their impoverished living environments. These cases are not considered learning disorders.

In an attempt to account for some of these factors, examination boards have worked on developing procedures that reflect differences in an individual's ethnic or cultural background. This is usually accomplished by using tests written specifically to the level of the test-taker's educational experience, or by using an examiner who is familiar with the individual's background.

READING DISORDERS

Dyslexic is a term that is often used but is not well understood by the general public. The word comes from two Greek words: *dys* (meaning difficulty) and *lexis* (words). A dyslexic literally has difficulty with words: reading, spelling, and writing.

Those with dyslexia cannot look at a word and learn it in the "normal" way. Children with dyslexia appear to have severe problems with the simplest rules of language. When a dyslexic looks at a word, he or she often sees it as a hodgepodge of letters, with no discernible shapes. For example, the child may struggle over words such as "it" and "the" or have trouble distinguishing between "from" and "form." Unfortunately, children suffering from any of the learning disorders are often labeled "dumb" by their peers, whereas, in fact, their intelligence level is usually the same as, if not higher than, that of their peers. The problem is that the child is unable to "learn how to learn" as other children do because what he or she sees makes no sense. Therefore, dyslexic children, whose impairment can range from mild to severe, require early identification and a suitable learning style in order to negotiate their school years with some degree of success. Even though early diagnosis can increase the likelihood of more productive lives for many with dyslexia, there is no known cure for learning disorders. An individual's success depends on the degree to which he or she learns to compensate for his or her disability.

Researchers have determined that 1 person in 25 is dyslexic. Dyslexia can be found among all economic classes and intelligence ranges of people. While the cause of dyslexia is unknown, it is believed to be caused by a combination of physiological, neurological, and genetic factors. Some studies indicate that a learning disorder can result from the failure of one side of the brain to gain dominance over the other side.

Unfortunately, many people simply regard children afflicted with a learning disorder as "slow learners." This is not true; many famous people, including Patton, Whoopi Goldberg, Walt Disney, and Albert Einstein, have achieved their amazing successes in spite of their learning disorders. In fact, some researchers believe that the same mental miscommunication that produces reading problems may also contribute to creative genius (Davis, 1997). Of course, not all children with dyslexia are geniuses, but most have average or above-average intelligence quotients (IQs).

Just like peers who do not have dyslexia, learning-disordered people display a wide variety of talents. For example, Patton was a military genius, Goldberg shines at performing arts, Disney excelled at visual arts, and Einstein was a scientific genius who won the Nobel Prize for physics. There are some basic mental functions, however, that many people with dyslexia share. They have a keen sense of their environment and show intense curiosity. These individuals are often highly intuitive and insightful. They think mainly in pictures instead of words, and they have vivid imaginations. If these basic abilities are encouraged and nurtured by parents and teachers, youngsters with learning disorders can grow into individuals of higher than normal intelligence and extraordinary creativity (Davis, 1997).

WHAT ARE THE SIGNS?

The essential feature of reading disorder is reading achievement—that is, accuracy, speed, and/or comprehension—that falls well below the average and significantly interferes with daily activities. When reading out loud, individuals with reading disorder are likely to distort, substitute, or omit letters and words. Whether reading out loud or silently, they tend to go slower than normal children of their age and education level, and often have trouble understanding what they're reading.

Symptoms of reading difficulty, such as an inability to distinguish between common letters or to associate common linguistic sounds (called *phonemes*) with letter symbols, may occur as early as kindergarten. However, a child is seldom diagnosed with reading disorder before the end of kindergarten or the beginning of first grade, as formal reading instruction usually doesn't begin until this point. The child can function at or near grade level in the early grades, particularly when his or her reading disorder is accompanied by a high IQ, and the reading disorder may not be fully apparent until the fourth grade or later. With early identification and intervention, the future is bright for most individuals, even though the underlying reading disorder persists into adult life.

HOW COMMON IS IT?

The prevalence of reading disorder in the United States is estimated to be four percent of school-age children. Sixty to eighty percent of the individuals diagnosed with reading disorder are male. The reason this

A teacher works on number reversals in a special education classroom with a student who has a mathematics disorder. About six percent of the population is believed to suffer from mathematics disorders.

percentage is so high may be because boys display disruptive behaviors in association with learning disorders more frequently. In essence, they call more attention to their disorders than do girls. Reading disorder runs in families and is quite common among siblings and parents of individuals with learning disorders.

The frequency with which reading disorder occurs is difficult to establish because many studies focus on the general occurrence of learning disorders without careful separation into the specific disorders of reading, mathematics, or written expression. Dyslexia—either alone or in combination with mathematics disorder or disorder of written expression—is believed to account for nearly four out of every five cases of learning disorder.

MATHEMATICS DISORDER

As its name implies, a mathematics disorder is characterized by mathematical ability that falls substantially below that expected for the individual's age and level of intelligence and education. Ability in mathematical calculation and reasoning is measured by performance on standardized tests. To be considered a mathematics disorder, the disturbance must be significant enough to interfere with academic achievement or daily activities that require mathematical skills.

Although symptoms of difficulty in mathematics, such as confusion in number concepts or an inability to count accurately, may appear as early as kindergarten or first grade, mathematics disorder is seldom diagnosed before the end of first grade. As with reading skills, this is typically because in most schools students don't receive sufficient formal mathematics instruction until this point. A child's mathematical disorder usually becomes evident by the time the student reaches second or third grade, although if the child has high intelligence, he or she may be able to function at or near the appropriate grade level in the early grades, with the mathematics disorder not becoming apparent until the fifth grade or later.

WHAT ARE THE SIGNS?

A student with mathematics disorder may experience a number of problems with different skills. Difficulties with vocabulary or linguistic skills—often caused by related dyslexia—affect the understanding or naming of mathematical terms, operations, or concepts, and the decoding of written problems into mathematical symbols. Perceptual skills may cause weaknesses in recognizing or reading numerical symbols or arithmetic signs and aligning numbers for calculations. And weak mathematical skills may create deficiencies in following sequences of mathematical steps, counting objects, and learning multiplication tables.

HOW COMMON IS IT?

Although mathematics disorder is generally not distinguished from the other learning disorders in prevalence studies, it is estimated that six percent of the school-age population is affected by mathematics disorder. The ratio of males to females is uncertain. As with other learning disorders, a large percentage of the diagnosed cases of mathematics disorder occur in lower socioeconomic classes.

DISORDER OF WRITTEN EXPRESSION

As with reading disorder and mathematics disorder, the disorder of written expression is marked by some basic criteria. Generally, writing skills fall substantially below those expected of individuals of the same age, relative to measured intelligence and education levels. And the disturbance in written expression must be severe enough to interfere with academic achievement or with common activities that require writing skills.

Difficulty in writing—particularly poor handwriting or copying ability, a problem writing certain letters correctly ("s" appears as "ƨ", for example), or an inability to remember letter sequences in common words—can appear as early as the first grade. However, disorder of written expression is rarely diagnosed before the end of first grade because students typically haven't received sufficient formal writing instruction until that point. The disorder is usually apparent by second grade.

WHAT ARE THE SIGNS?

Generally, there is a combination of difficulties in the individual's ability to compose written texts. These difficulties can include grammatical or punctuation errors within sentences, poor paragraph organization, multiple spelling errors, and excessively poor handwriting. The diagnosis is generally not made if there are only spelling errors or poor handwriting in the absence of other forms of impairment in written expression. Compared with other learning disorders, relatively little is known about writing disorder and its treatment, particularly when it occurs in the absence of reading disorder.

Except for spelling, standardized tests in this area are less well developed than tests of reading or mathematical ability. For this reason, an evaluation of impairment in written skill may include a comparison between numerous samples of a youngster's written schoolwork and expected performance for age and IQ. This is especially the case for young children in the early elementary grades. For teachers or clinicians to establish the presence and extent of this disorder, they might ask a child to complete a number of tasks—including copying, writing to dictation, and writing spontaneously.

HOW COMMON IS IT?

Disorder of written expression is sometimes accompanied by problems with language and eye-to-hand coordination. Writing disorder is also commonly found in combination with reading disorder or mathematics disorder. However, just how frequently it occurs is difficult to establish, as many studies focus on the occurrence of learning disorders in general without separation into specific types. It is known that disorder of written expression rarely occurs without other learning disorders.

With patience and understanding, teachers can help learning-disordered students overcome their problems.

2

HISTORY OF
LEARNING DISORDERS

The work of neurologist Dr. Samuel T. Orton first brought dyslexia to the attention of American educators and doctors in the 1920s. For decades thereafter, however, the general public still viewed children who had difficulty learning as either emotionally disturbed, mentally retarded, or culturally disadvantaged.

In the early 1940s, researchers began to identify a fourth possible explanation for learning difficulties: a neurobiological disorder. Early research suggested that these problems were caused by brain damage. Because children with dyslexic problems looked "normal," it was concluded that the brain damage must be slight or minimal. Thus, the earliest label for these children was "minimal brain damage."

Additional observations and studies, however, revealed no evidence of brain damage. Instead, it became evident that the difficulty was with the way the brain functioned. All of the brain mechanisms were present and operable, but some of the "wiring" did not function the way it should. To move away from the idea of brain damage and to reflect this concept of faulty functioning, the term "minimal brain dysfunction" was introduced in 1966 (Silver, 1995).

Researchers began to study these dysfunctions and introduced concepts and terms for each of the observed academic disabilities. Initially, the basic area of difficulty was defined using existing terms. Thus, a problem with reading was called "dyslexia," a word derived from the Greek *dys*, meaning poor or inadequate, and *lexis*, meaning words or language. Likewise, a difficulty with writing was dubbed "dysgraphia," and a problem with arithmetic was labeled "dyscalculia." Later, an effort was made to clarify the specific learning difficulties that caused problems with reading, writing, and arithmetic. The focus shifted to the concept of specific "learning disabilities," and a child with such problems was called "learning disabled" (Silver, 1995).

Attempts to understand specifically how learning disorders develop have been aided in recent years by technology that looks at brain activity. A procedure called functional magnetic resonance neuroimaging allows researchers to examine pictures of learning-disabled brains and compare them with nonimpaired brains. This allows them to see whether the brain of a person with a learning disorder is different than the brain of a person who learns normally. A number of studies have found variations in brain size and shape and have found certain malformations in specific regions of the brains of people with learning disorders. However, these observations are still not widely accepted as the causes of learning disorders; more research is required for them to be so established (Lyon, 1995).

FAMILY INFLUENCE

The hypothesis that learning disabilities are handed down from generation to generation has been examined for nearly a century. The possibility that reading disability might run in families was noted as early as 1907. Over the following decades, numerous reports were written describing cases of dyslexia that spanned several generations. These reports revealed that a variety of severe difficulties in areas such as reading recognition and reading comprehension was often shared by parents and siblings of those already diagnosed with dyslexia (Cook and Leventhal, 1992). The symptoms of mathematics and writing disorders, such as weak counting ability and poor spelling, were generally considered to be part of reading disorder until decades later, when reading, mathematics, and writing disorders were classified as three distinct types of learning disorders.

As researchers conducted more studies, they found that even though a parent and a child might both have a learning disability, each individual might suffer from a different type. For instance, a parent who struggled mainly with disorder of written expression might have a child who had greater difficulty with reading disorder. This led researchers in the field of psychiatry to consider possibilities other than genetic inheritance as the reason that learning disorders tended to run in families. Researchers continue to explore a variety of causes—familial and environmental—to determine what has the greatest influence over the occurrence of the disorders (Neuwirth, 1993).

Children with learning disorders may have trouble with problem solving or recognizing patterns.

EDUCATIONAL RESPONSE

As the psychiatric profession gained more knowledge about learning disabilities, parents and educational institutions also became more enlightened. Students who were once considered mentally retarded were now seen as individuals with normal or high intelligence in need of customized teaching methods.

In response to this need in 1926, the Gow School was founded just outside of Buffalo, New York. This private school was established specifically for boys who were of normal—or higher—intelligence but had trouble with reading and writing, to help them prepare for college (Rogers, 1991). Other schools for children with learning disorders soon followed. These schools were expensive, however, and those who couldn't afford a private school had to rely on the public school system, which was a lot slower to properly accommodate—and had fewer resources to help—those with learning disorders. And, unfortunately, those public schools that did provide special instruction were generally criticized for offering inadequate classes (Staples, 1997).

In 1975, the federal government stepped in to support the individualized approach with the Education for All Handicapped Children Act. Later revised and renamed the Individuals with Disabilities Education Act (IDEA), the law ordered states to provide disabled children—including those with learning disorders—"a free, appropriate public education."

Since the enactment of IDEA, children with learning disorders have generally benefited from a variety of teaching methods designed to accommodate their needs. Many of these children blossomed under the establishment of special education classes, where they received the individual instruction they needed. Unfortunately, much of the 1980s saw a large increase in the number of children diagnosed as learning disabled. Much of this increase has been explained by the switch from traditional methods for teaching language skills—especially phonics, which uses sound-letter-word construction drills—to the less-structured whole language approach, which encourages students to wander through stories, devising creative spellings when they need to. The debate over which teaching method is more effective continues today.

Another controversial issue that affects children with learning disorders, their families, and their teachers is the question of what classroom setting provides the best learning environment for these students. Some educators believe in the established concept of separating students with learning disorders from other students of their grade level in special education classrooms, where they can receive more individualized treatment. A newer concept that is being instituted in more and more public schools is "mainstreaming." In this practice, students with learning disorders are placed into the regular student classrooms.

This move toward mainstreaming, also called "inclusion" by educators, began with a report (Heller, Holtzman, and Messick, 1982) issued

HELPING STUDENTS OVERCOME LEARNING DISORDERS: THE LANDMARK SCHOOL

The Landmark School, an institution created to work exclusively with children who have dyslexia or other learning disorders, was founded in 1971 by the Learning Disabilities Foundation (now called the Landmark Foundation) in Prides Crossing, Massachusetts. The school now has over 500 students enrolled in Massachusetts and at a second campus in Encino, California, and has developed programs for students at all age levels.

Landmark accepts only students who have been diagnosed with learning disorders, and who are of average or above-average intelligence. The goal of the school is to help these children overcome their learning disorders and reach their full potential so that they can go on to a career or a college education in a "normal" setting. Approximately 80 percent of all Landmark graduates go on to enter college.

The focus of the academic program at Landmark is on small classes and individualized attention. Most programs feature daily one-on-one instruction with a tutor for part of the day, and small classes (averaging six students) to ensure that each student receives the attention that he or she needs. Emphasis is placed on the development of language and communications skills, including vocabulary, reading, written expression, and oral expression. Students also learn other traditional school subjects, including mathematics, science, social studies, and study skills. Electives and extracurricular activities such as sports, art, and drama are also provided, encouraging the students to express their creativity and their talents outside the classroom as well.

Additionally, special programs are available for students who need extra help in expressing themselves, or for those older students who wish to prepare themselves for a job or to enter college. Vocational courses in the fields of auto mechanics, woodworking, and home mechanics are offered, leading to careers such as auto repair, boat building, plumbing, and electrical repair. The preparatory and pre-college programs are designed to enable students to become independent learners and hone the skills they will need to be successful in a college setting. Almost all graduates of the preparatory program go on to attend college.

Whatever the students choose to do when they graduate, the goal of all the Landmark programs is to give them the skills and confidence they need for success. Landmark's track record has shown that learning-disordered students can go on to successful careers in many different fields, if they learn at an early age not to allow their disorders to stop them.

by the National Academy of Sciences, which found that the classification and placement of children into special education classrooms was "ineffective and discriminatory." The report recommended that "children be given noninclusive or extra-class placement for special services only if (a) they can be accurately classified, and only if (b) noninclusion demonstrates superior results." Eventually, federal legislation mandated that all public-school students must be educated in the "least restrictive environment."

Although critics of mainstreaming argue that children with learning disabilities and others traditionally taught in a special education classroom would not keep up with unimpaired students in a normal classroom setting, the conclusions of several important studies (Baker, 1994; Baker, Wang et al., 1985; and Carlberg and Kavale, 1980) indicated that inclusive education has a moderate beneficial effect on the academic and social outcomes of students with disabilities. Another study (Staub and Peck, 1995) found that non-disabled students were also not affected negatively by the incorporation of "special needs" students into their classroom. Despite this evidence, the issue of mainstreaming vs. special education continues to be discussed (Tanner, 1995; Staples, 1997).

Children with learning disorders frequently feel alienated or frustrated by their problems in school; they may come to believe that they are "dumb" or "slow."

3

HOW INDIVIDUALS ARE AFFECTED

L earning disorders affect children of all cultural backgrounds and intelligence levels. It strikes those who were read to as infants as well as those who grew up without a book in sight. Reading disorder is the most common learning disorder, but it typically occurs in conjunction with mathematics disorder and disorder of written expression.

Children with learning disorders often absorb thoughtless comments by peers. They may define themselves in light of their disabilities, as "slow," "different," or even "airheaded." Sometimes they don't know how they're different, but they know how awful they feel. Their tension or shame can lead them to act out in various ways, such as belligerence and fighting. Or, they may become isolated and depressed. They may even stop trying to learn and achieve, and eventually drop out of school (Neuwirth, 1993).

Children with learning disabilities and attention disorders may have trouble making friends with peers. In many cases, this may be because poor classroom performance results in ostracism by other students, who label the learning-disabled child "stupid." Other children with learning disorders may find that they are are more comfortable with younger children, whose skills are at their lower level. Some children have a hard time interpreting "social cues," such as tone of voice or facial expressions; misunderstanding various situations, they tend to act inappropriately, which turns others away.

Without professional help, the child's situation can spiral out of control. The more that children or teenagers fail, the more frustrated they become, and the more damage is done to their self-esteem. If they act in a disruptive manner as a result of their frustration, the ensuing punishment will do nothing to eliminate feelings of failure and low self-esteem (Neuwirth, 1993).

THE IMPORTANCE OF DIAGNOSIS

A child's learning disorder typically becomes apparent during grade school, when basic skills, attention, and motivation become building blocks for subsequent learning. Children who have problems in these areas often need special instruction. In later school years, weak organizational skills can cause significant problems with note taking, time management, and book and paper arrangements—even if other basic skills have been mastered. In high school and college, students who have not mastered these basic skills will have difficulty learning foreign languages, writing efficiently, or reading for pleasure (Popper and Steingard, 1994).

Children with learning disorders whose problems go undiagnosed tend to have problems in public schools. Some grow ashamed of their failure and act out in class or become truant. The fortunate ones are those identified early and given special education or sent to private schools where teachers drill them in the fundamentals of language. Fortunately for Dennis, whose experience is highlighted in the following case report, he was diagnosed early enough to overcome his difficulties with reading and writing.

■   ■   ■

Dennis had always been an overactive boy, sometimes jumping on the sofa for hours until he collapsed with exhaustion. In grade school, he never sat still and repeatedly interrupted lessons. But he was a friendly, well-meaning child, so adults didn't get too angry with him. His academic problems became evident in third grade, when his teacher realized that Dennis could recognize only a few words and wrote like a first-grader. She recommended that Dennis repeat the third grade to give him a chance to catch up. After another full year, however, his behavior was still out of control, and his reading and writing had not improved.

In fifth grade, Dennis's teacher sent him to the school psychologist for testing. Dennis was diagnosed as having developmental reading and writing disorders as well as attention-deficit disorder with hyperactivity. He was placed in an all-day special education program, where he could get individual attention for his particular problems. His family doctor prescribed the medication Ritalin (methylphenidate) to reduce his hyperactivity and distractibility. Along with working to improve his

In some cases, children or teens with learning disorders "act out" their frustration through disruptive or illegal behaviors such as shoplifting.

reading, the special education teacher helped him to improve his listening skills. Since his handwriting was still poor, he learned to type homework assignments and reports on a computer. At age 19, Dennis graduated from high school and was accepted by a college that gives special assistance to students with learning disabilities. With the help of lectures and tape-recorded textbooks, he graduated from college.

Dennis is now 23 years old and still seems to have too much energy. But that hasn't stopped him from pursuing a career in electronics. Dennis is also getting married soon, and, though he and his fiancée are

A dyslexic student works on a writing exercise, illustrating the difficulty dyslexics have with transposing letters and reversing or mirror-imaging them.

concerned that their children might have a learning disorder, they know it can be mastered (Neuwirth, 1993).

■   ■   ■

Dennis's case illustrates the great potential for those with learning disorders, and it also emphasizes the critical role teachers play in identifying and acting on the possibility of such disorders. Further, Dennis's story touches on the common occurrence of accompanying disorders, such as attention-deficit/hyperactivity disorder (ADHD). We will address disorders that typically occur simultaneously with learning disabilities in the section "Coexistence with Other Disorders."

THE EVALUATION PROCESS

Most children with learning disabilities are diagnosed in elementary school, where the problem usually surfaces first. Students who are having obvious problems are given a variety of tests to determine if, in fact, they have dyslexia or another learning disorder. Some of these tests measure native intelligence, or IQ; some measure school achievement; and others tests measure emotional levels.

The process of diagnosing and evaluating a learning disability does not have much in common with, say, reading an X ray to determine whether or not a bone is broken. Intelligence and achievement tests can only provide a general measure of ability and future performance. These tests results must be combined with a close and accurate assessment by a teacher. If a learning disorder is suspected, a medical and psychological evaluation are necessary to determine if a problem actually exists. The final evaluation is usually based on the conclusions of a diagnostic team, rather than just one person's judgement.

Although the diagnostic process is far from perfect, it has several benefits. An early diagnosis will enable a child with a learning disorder to get help before becoming frustrated and giving up on school. This is critical to future success in overcoming the disorder. Also, the tests often help children with learning disorders—a weakness—learn about strengths the child did not realize he or she possessed, such as artistic or musical talent. This knowledge will help build the child's self-esteem.

The law requires that all children with educational disabilities be reevaluated every three years. The results of these retests are compared with previous tests so that improvements can be recorded. Other factors may affect improvement. For example, as school anxiety lessens, or a family crisis is resolved, a child may show greater aptitude.

THE EFFECTS OF READING DISORDER

In order to grasp how reading disabilities affect a person, it's helpful to understand the reading process. Basically, reading requires two tasks: decoding, or word recognition, and comprehension. Decoding is the mental process of transcribing a printed word into speech, and comprehension involves interpreting the message or meaning of the text. The decoding process is unique to reading and different from the recognition of spoken words, whereas the linguistic skills underlying reading comprehension are the same for both reading and listening (Silver, 1995).

Generally, reading disabilities occur in one of three ways. Most stu-

LEARNING DISORDERS AND ATTENTION DEFICIT/ HYPERACTIVITY DISORDER

A ttention deficit/hyperactivity disorder (ADHD) is the most common disorder observed in conjunction with learning disorders. It typically appears with reading disorders, although it has been seen with other learning disorders as well. Children with ADHD have trouble paying attention to any one thing for a long period of time, and/or exhibit hyperactive behavior. Frequently, they are also easily irritated. These behaviors, like learning disorders, make it hard for these children to perform well in school and can cause many of the same negative repercussions. For example, a boy with ADHD who becomes a "class clown" because he has difficulty paying attention to the teacher may be labeled a troublemaker, just as he

would if he were using his clowning behavior to "act out" or draw attention away from his learning disorder. Whereas children with learning disorders are often considered "slow" or "dumb" by others who do not understand their problems, children suffering from ADHD or related behavioral disorders are told they are "disrespectful," "bad" kids because of their difficulties behaving appropriately for the classroom environment. In both cases, people who do not understand the disorders tend to blame the students, believing—incorrectly—that they should be able to just "get over it."

Facing similar problems, children with ADHD are helped by some of the same teaching strategies used with learning-disordered children. One-on-one, personalized attention seems to help them focus and understand material, and many students show improvement in a "resource room" setting, where they can participate in varied activities to help them learn. With this kind of directed attention, they can learn the social, academic, and organizational skills they need to be able to become successful in their adult lives. Adults with ADHD learn to structure their working environments very simply, so that they have fewer things to distract them when they are trying to concentrate on single tasks, just as adults with learning disorders learn how to approach the subjects that give them trouble in different ways, allotting extra time if necessary and employing creative problem-solving strategies. One difference between the two conditions is that treatment of ADHD also frequently involves stimulants such as methylphenidate (marketed under the name Ritalin), whereas learning disorders are not normally treatable with medication.

Doctors are still not sure exactly what causes ADHD, or how it is related to learning disorders. Some research indicates that both problems may be related to changes in the way that neurons connect in the brain, and children with certain risk factors—such as alcohol use by their mothers during the later part of pregnancy—are more likely to have one or both conditions. As research continues, scientists hope to further understand how ADHD and learning disorders develop, and find new ways to approach treatment so that people with learning disorders or ADHD can live normal, happy lives.

A boy in a special education classroom uses physical objects to help him grasp the mathematical concepts he is studying.

dents with developmental reading disorder have difficulty—sometimes extreme difficulty—with word recognition but not with comprehension. Spelling, because it uses the same skill as word recognition, is also frequently impaired. A second and relatively rare problem is hyperlexia (the reverse of dyslexia), in which comprehension is limited but decoding is not generally a problem. Students with this problem can read almost any text but do not always understand it. Third, both decoding and comprehension can be impaired, resulting in what is sometimes called "reading backwardness" (Silver, 1995).

Commonly, individuals with reading disorder have difficulty translating letters into words and reading them aloud. They also often have problems with left-right orientation, hearing spoken sounds properly, and eye-hand coordination. When reading, they tend to switch letters, such as "b" with "d," and transpose words, like "saw" for "was."

Individuals with reading disabilities may also omit letters, as in reading "bread" as "bead," and substitute letters, where "bread" becomes "broad."

Nearly everyone with a reading disorder has problems with spelling, and these difficulties may be more severe and long lasting than the reading problem itself. A large majority experience speech difficulties. Many also have disorder of written expression, hearing problems, and poor handwriting. These children may be uncoordinated. Difficulty with attention span is also common, compounding problems in reading and language (Popper and Steingard, 1994).

COEXISTENCE WITH OTHER DISORDERS

A psychological condition affecting school-age children called attention-deficit/hyperactivity disorder (ADHD) often appears in conjunction with reading disabilities. In fact, the two appear so frequently together that over the years some researchers have wondered if one disorder causes the other. The frequency of learning disorders and ADHD has also created difficulty for researchers in determining whether negative behavior is caused by the learning disorder, the attention-deficit disorder, or both in combination.

About 25 percent of children diagnosed primarily with reading disorder also have a psychological condition known as conduct disorder. Conduct disorder is indicated by a child's constant and extreme defiance of rules and authority figures, and is usually evident before a child reaches adolescence. Approximately one-third of the children whose primary diagnosis is conduct disorder also have some level of reading disorder as well (Spencer, 1996).

In very young children, there sometimes appears a serious problem that the American Psychiatric Association calls "communications disorders." A person with a communication disorder may have a problem expressing himself or herself because of undeveloped verbal language skills (this is called expressive language disorder), or may have a problem understanding verbal instructions (mixed receptive-expressive language disorder). The category also includes some hearing problems, as well as stuttering. The APA's *Diagnostic and Statistical Manual of Mental Disorders*, 4th edition (*DSM-IV*) indicates that both communication disorders and learning disorders are caused by the same problems in the brain.

Typically, these communication disorders are recognizable before a child is three years old. However, although communication disorders and learning disorders traditionally have been viewed as two distinct development problems, there is some evidence that problems like expressive language disorder actually may be an early stage of learning disorder (Popper and Steingard, 1994).

Children suffering from such neurological disorders as Tourette's syndrome (which causes inadvertant physical tics and vocal outbursts, such as uncontrolled swearing), neurofibromatosis (developmental changes in the nervous system, muscles, bones, or skin marked with the formation of skin tumors), or seizure disorders such as epilepsy show a higher-than-expected incidence of learning disorders (Popper and Steingard, 1994).

Coping with a learning disorder is difficult enough; most learning-disabled children and adolescents who also suffer from ADHD or another disorder battle emotional problems and have trouble with relationships at school and at home, especially when disruptive behavior problems such as ADHD or conduct disorder are added to the mix (Popper and Steingard, 1994; Silver, 1995).

POTENTIAL OUTCOME

A child diagnosed with reading disorder is likely to experience a lifetime of associated effects. Dyslexia commonly leads to low self-esteem in childhood, difficulty with traditional learning structures in adolescence, and underachievement in adulthood. How well a person is doing by adulthood greatly depends on the individual's personality as well as the attitudes and actions of family members, teachers, and other nurturing influences.

Slow development of reading skills is usually identified in grade school. Typically, by the third grade children with reading disorder are one to two years behind in their development. At this point, special instruction is usually needed to bring these children up to the reading level of their classmates. In adolescence, they may learn foreign languages at a slower pace and still struggle with reading. Frustrated with their performance, some students lose interest in school, and possibly even drop out; many show more frequent signs of disruptive behavior disorders. As a result, as adults they're likely to work at unskilled jobs and deal with periodic unemployment (Popper and Steingard, 1994).

Some adults with dyslexia never attain substantial reading skills and may adapt by hiding their disability from their children, friends, and employers. Although embarrassed by their lack of skills, they may not seek further education and will continue to resist seeking guidance. Such resistance is a major contributor to persistent reading problems. By not addressing a major learning problem early on, a person is likely to develop poor methods for handling other significant problems later in life (Popper and Steingard, 1994).

THE EFFECTS OF MATHEMATICS DISORDER

For persons to function independently in our society, they must be able to make simple mathematical calculations. Logical reasoning, arithmetic, calculation of fractions, decimals, and percentages—as well as measurement of space, time, and weight—are basic skills.

Individuals with mathematics disorder have difficulty learning to count, solving basic mathematical problems, conceptualizing sets of objects, and thinking spatially (for example, right-left or up-down). They may also have problems with mathematical memory and number order, with copying shapes, and with naming mathematical signs and concepts. Typically, some reading and spelling problems are seen in association with mathematics disorder.

During a child's early school years, difficulties usually increase only gradually, because mathematical skills are based on the developmental completion of earlier steps. However, some children with mathematics disorder may perform well on basic arithmetic and fail later in trigonometry and geometry, subjects that require highly abstract and spatial thinking. Whereas most individuals show gradual improvement, potential problems associated with mathematics disorder include low self-esteem, truancy, dropping out of school, and disruptive behaviors (Popper and Steingard, 1994).

If a mathematics disorder is recognized, and a proper educational program developed, however, children with this disorder have a bright future. The following vignette illustrates how some are capable of discovering hidden and unexpected talents once they are properly diagnosed and taught how to manage their learning disorder.

■   ■   ■

When Susan was a child, she was so withdrawn that people sometimes forgot she was there. She seemed to drift in a world of her own. When she did speak, she often called objects by the wrong names. She had few friends and played mostly with dolls or her younger sister. In school, Susan hated reading and math because none of the letters, numbers, or plus and minus signs made any sense. She felt awful about herself. She'd been told—and was convinced—that she was retarded.

By the time Susan was promoted to the sixth grade, she still couldn't do basic math. Her mother brought her to a private clinic for testing. The clinician observed that Susan had trouble associating symbols with their meaning, and this was holding back her language, reading, and math development. Susan called objects by the wrong words and could not associate sounds with letters or recognize math symbols. However, Susan's IQ of 128 meant that she was quite intelligent. In addition to developing an individualized education plan (IEP), the clinician recommended that Susan receive counseling for her low self-esteem and depression.

Now age 14, Susan still tends to be quiet, but she is in ninth grade and enjoys learning. Thankfully, she no longer believes she's retarded, and her use of words has improved. With her newly gained confidence, Susan has become a talented craftsperson and loves making clothes and furniture for her sister's dolls. Although she remains in a special education program, she is making slow but steady progress in reading and math (Neuwirth, 1993).

■   ■   ■

Perhaps one of the best outcomes of Susan's counseling is her optimistic attitude. She now has a reason to believe that she can do almost anything—she is not retarded, or "dumb." Often a person with learning disorders is highly intelligent, like Susan, and all he or she needs are the tools, including confidence, to master the disorder.

Generally, the symptoms of mathematics disorder are not as noticeable as those of other disorders. Weaknesses in one's ability to do arithmetic do not typically stigmatize children socially and may not therefore be a direct source of personal distress. As they go through adolescence and into adulthood, individuals with mathematics disorder may experience less stress than those with a reading or writing disorder. This is largely because the mathematical skills of a normal fifth- or sixth-grader are quite sufficient for most adults to perform common, day-to-day calculations. In fact, it is likely that this disorder may exist quietly in many adults, who make accommodations in their lives and work to manage the dysfunctions that were more evident during their school years (Popper and Steingard, 1994).

THE EFFECTS OF DISORDER OF WRITTEN EXPRESSION

Compared to reading disorder and mathematics disorder, the disorder of written expression is not well documented as a distinct learning disability. Likewise, assessment and specific plans to treat this problem are not as well developed. Like individuals with other learning disorders, those with writing disorder tend to experience problems with self-esteem and disruptive behavior.

Children with writing disorder may exhibit certain symptoms—including poor handwriting and copying ability and difficulty remembering letter sequences in common words—as early as the first grade. Individuals with writing disorder tend to reveal their difficulty with expressive writing through slowness and low volume output, illegibility, and letter reversals. The most common problem areas include spelling, grammar, sentence and paragraph formation, and punctuation. The struggle to find the right word or to organize a sentence often results in multiple erasures, rewritings, and spacing errors. Intellectual ability to perceive substantial meaning and understand abstract ideas also may be limited. Because of these difficulties, a student with disorder of written expression may refuse to complete work or submit assignments and repeatedly do poorly on much of the work that is handed in (Popper and Steingard, 1994).

Dyslexia

It was bad for me in catholic school. I was in first grade! I did that I was stopit. I left school for reding I come back and forth every day. It was not good at all. It help a little. I came out after school and I came in cry. Because kids said I was stopit and call my name. I did not have any freind. But my brother. I was not shor about him to. Then my bother fond it that I was speshel. Then I had more and more freinds. It was hard! Always I wanted to kill my self. But 3 year agg it chang I came to Landmark. I did not want to kill my self. It has help me alot.

This boy's essay about his problems with dyslexia reflects both the difficulty he has with writing and also the emotional pain his disorder has caused him.

4

THE IMPACT ON SOCIETY

earning disorders have become a problem of significant proportion.
Every year, 120,000 additional students are found to have learning disabilities; the U.S. Department of Education reported that 2.4 million
school children in the United States received special education for their learning disorders during the 1993–94 school year. This number comprises approximately four percent of U.S. pupils, and probably falls short of the actual number of those struggling with learning disorders. Thousands of children are
never properly diagnosed or treated, or fall between the cracks because they
are not deemed eligible for special education services (Neuwirth, 1993).

Learning disorders do not affect only the students who have them. The consequences of not properly identifying and addressing learning disabilities are
shared by every major institution in the country. Without proper training or
funding, schools face the enormous challenge of meeting the needs of their
students with disabilities. Businesses are affected, in turn, by the diminishing
pool of trained and skilled workers. In addition, state and federal government
agencies are often called upon for assistance—usually monetary and sometimes in the form of employment opportunities—to help reduce the burden
on society. Any assistance they provide is afforded only by an increased financial burden on taxpayers. And the criminal justice system is sometimes left to
handle the high number of adults who were never properly diagnosed or
treated for learning disabilities when they were children.

In an effort to address such problems, the U.S. federal government has ini-
tiated some reform of the education options available to those with learning
disorders. With the enactment of the Education for All Handicapped Children
Act of 1975 and its revision, Individuals with Disabilities Education Act

OVERCOMING A LEARNING DISORDER: THOMAS EDISON

Thomas Alva Edison, one of the most prolific and well-known inventors the United States has ever produced, was born in 1847, the youngest of seven children. His only formal education, when he was seven years old, lasted for three months; his teacher pronounced him "addled," and said that he would never amount to anything because of his inability to learn in a classroom environment.

Edison's mother, fortunately, did not accept the teacher's judgment. Herself a former schoolteacher, she taught her youngest child at home, answering his endless questions and encouraging him to do hands-on work that helped him to grasp scientific concepts. Although learning disorders were not understood then, research since Edison's time has shown that the creative, hands-on methods his mother used to help him learn are often the best ways for children with learning disorders to realize their potential. The creativity and experimental technique that Edison learned at this young age would help him throughout his life and career.

Edison's first two inventions—an electric vote counter and a modified stock ticker—did not bring him much success, but after he moved to New York in 1869, he managed to establish a reputation as a man who was good at improving designs that others had begun and perfecting devices that others had not been able to make efficient. Eventually, he set up his own laboratory in Menlo Park, New Jersey, where he could work on inventions full-time.

Edison's lab was the first industrial research laboratory; he employed a scientific team to help him test ideas and improve designs for useful—and sometimes revolutionary—inventions. At times, Edison would stay up for as many as five days straight, with only brief naps to keep up his strength, while he worked on an idea that challenged his inventiveness. Edison's Menlo Park team improved telephone technology, which led to Edison's favorite invention, the phonograph. This allowed reproduction of sound for the first time, and has been considered Edison's most original invention.

The most famous invention to come out of the Menlo Park lab was the electric lighting system. Others had experimented with incandescent lamps, but Edison was the first to envision a complete system of lamps and electrical distribution that could compete with the gaslight system popular in the late 19th century. With the help of his assistants, Edison designed a light bulb suitable for commercial use, and found several ways to cut the costs of supplying electricity. By 1882, he had set up a commercial electrical enterprise, lighting homes for 85 customers from a central

station on Pearl Street in New York City.

Throughout his life, Edison never stopped working on ways to improve his inventions or come up with new ones. After the electric light venture proved successful, Edison went on to invent a moving-picture camera and a peepshow device called the kinetoscope to show what the camera had recorded. Toward the end of his life, he tested new methods for manufacturing chemicals and cement, and looked for economical ways to obtain rubber from plants native to the United States. By the time of his death in 1931, Edison had seen his most promising inventions and ideas radically change the way people lived. The boy who "would never amount to anything" had become an inventor who changed the world.

Students with learning disabilities are unlikely to receive the attention they need in large classrooms. One problem with "mainstreaming" students—moving them out of special education classes and into regular classrooms—is that less than one-quarter of teachers know how to teach reading to children with a reading disorder.

(IDEA), special education programs have become widespread. These programs have helped some individuals with learning disorders go on to additional education and/or successful careers. However, although such programs have helped many people with learning disorders, many school systems argue that their efforts to develop such programs in compliance with federal law have become too expensive. Also, despite the expense and effort, studies based on government data show that a large percentage of learning-disabled children continue to leave school without diplomas. A significant number of this group end up in jail soon thereafter (Staples, 1997). No optimal solution has yet been found,

DO YOU HAVE A LEARNING DISABILITY?

D o you wonder if you have a learning disability? If you have reached high school without the assistance of special education classes or tutorial help, the chances are good that any problem you have is a mild one. Most of the reasons for academic problems in high school are not related to learning disabilities. Poor study habits, heavy academic loads, difficult subject matter, too many extracurricular activities, and personal or family stress are more often to blame. On the other hand, if you are having serious academic difficulty no matter how hard you study, you may have an undiagnosed disability.

The most frequently displayed symptoms of learning disabilities are listed here. Most of us exhibit a few of these characteristics at one time or another. But the persistence of a cluster of these problems could signify a learning disability.

- Short attention span, easily distracted
- Restless hyperactivity
- Poor letter or word memory
- Poor auditory memory
- Inability to discriminate between letters, numbers, or sounds
- Poor handwriting
- Reads poorly, if at all
- Cannot follow multiple directions
- Erratic performance from day to day
- Impulsive
- Poor coordination
- Late gross or fine motor development
- Difficulty telling time or distinguishing left from right
- Late speech development, immature speech
- Trouble understanding words or concepts
- Trouble naming familiar people or things
- Says one thing, means another
- Responds inappropriately in many instances
- Adjusts poorly to change

Source: The Association for Children and Adults with Learning Disabilities

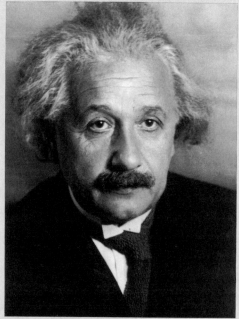

Whoopi Goldberg and Albert Einstein have shown through their examples that people with learning disorders can accomplish their goals and lead creative, successful lives.

and government and education groups continue to search for viable alternatives.

Another of the ways that learning disorders affect society is a result of the controversial issue discussed in Chapter 2: mainstreaming vs. special education. One of the strongest arguments against mainstreaming is that less than a quarter of American teachers know how to teach reading to children who have been diagnosed with dyslexia. To truly be successful, mainstreaming would require a huge effort to retrain teachers currently working in public schools; this would cost taxpayers more money. In addition, fundamental changes would be needed at colleges and universities that train teachers (Staples, 1997). The question remains whether it is more effective—in terms of time, money, and the potential positive contributions of those with learning disorders—to develop retraining programs so that teachers can better assist learning-disabled students, or to continue to devise ways of handling problems associated with having a segment of the population that is unable to read or do basic mathematics.

The good news is that individuals with learning disorders can contribute greatly to society, if they are given the proper education and family support. Many people who suffer from dyslexia or other learning problems have great promise, as the contributions of geniuses such as Albert Einstein or talented performers like Whoopi Goldberg prove. Nevertheless, the impact of learning disorders on society is largely measured in negative terms: the cost in dollars to educate, train, or rehabilitate such individuals. Unfortunately, educational solutions are ultimately based on school budgets and government subsidies, and today many states are placing stricter limits on spending for special education. For opportunities to improve for children with learning disorders—and for those children to have a chance to make a positive mark on society—teachers, educational institutions, researchers, medical professionals, and the government will have to work together to find better solutions.

One thing is certain: society will be faced with questions about the impact of learning disorders for quite some time, as the number of people diagnosed with learning disorders continues to increase.

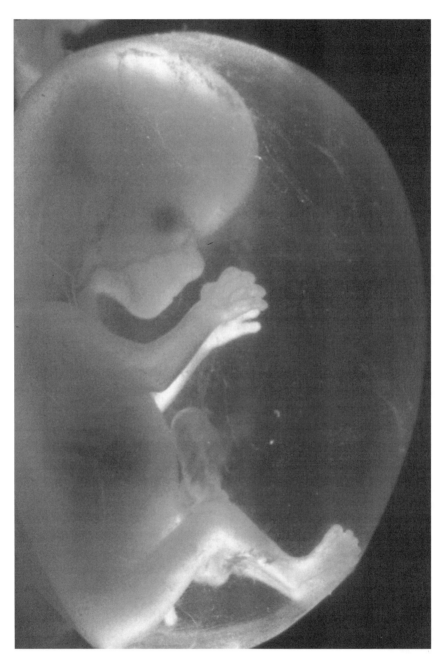

The human fetus is extremely vulnerable. If its development is disrupted during the later part of pregnancy, neurons in the brain may not connect normally, leading to learning disorders or other problems.

5

FINDING THE CAUSES

A lthough doctors are beginning to understand why some people have problems reading or learning, the cause of learning disorders remains unknown. Actually, there are many potential causes, although the main problem appear to be neurological, or involving the brain. There is a segment in the brain that controls language development; if this area is underdeveloped, or dysfunctional (meaning it does not work correctly), reading disorder, mathematics disorder, and writing disorder can result (Strub and Wise, 1992).

NEUROLOGICAL DEVELOPMENT

As a fetus forms in the mother's womb, its brain develops from a few cells into a complex organ made of billions of specialized, interconnected nerve cells called neurons. In the early stages of pregnancy, the brain stem forms to control basic life functions such as breathing and digestion. Later, a deep ridge divides the cerebrum, which is the thinking part of the brain, into right and left hemispheres. Finally, the areas involved with processing sight, sound, and other senses develop, as do the areas associated with attention, thinking, and emotion.

Throughout pregnancy, this brain development is vulnerable to disruptions. Things can go wrong that may alter how the neurons form or interconnect. If a disruption occurs early, the fetus may die, or the infant may be born with widespread disabilities and possible mental retardation. If the disruption occurs later, when the cells are becoming specialized and moving into place, it may leave errors in the cell makeup, location, or connections. It is believed that these errors, affecting the way areas of the brain communicate, may later show up as learning disorders (Neuwirth, 1993).

In an attempt to understand the specific neurological causes of learning

Some research has suggested that there is a genetic basis for learning disorders, or that parents who have learning disorders may not provide good models for their children to learn how to use language or mathematics.

disorders, researchers study the brain activity of individuals with learning disorders and compare it to that of individuals who learn normally. Functional magnetic resonance neuroimaging is one method they use to observe brain activity. This noninvasive technology involves taking detailed "pictures" of the brain that measure levels of activity in various areas of the cerebrum. These would be taken while a child with a learning disorder attempts to read, and the information is then compared to results from a child who is not learning disabled (Lyon, 1995). Researchers can draw conclusions about the areas of the brain that cause or influence learning problems based on the differences between these brain images.

Imaging technology has provided the first look at where phonological processing, the basis of reading, takes place in the central nervous system. It also has provided visual proof to support decades-old theories about the cause of certain symptoms. Clinicians who work with reading-disabled patients have repeatedly seen problems with language ability, attention, and memory as abnormalities in thought processing. Neuroimaging has shown that in many cases the areas of the brain responsible for phonological processing do indeed behave differently in reading-disabled individuals than they do in those who read well (Lyon, 1995).

Although neurological conditions are the most commonly accepted causes of learning disorders, many other factors can contribute to their origin and severity. Family history of learning disorders, or other syndromes such as ADHD, greatly affects the severity of one or both of these disorders in a child. Frequently, learning disorders are also accompanied and exacerbated by a number of general medical conditions surrounding pregnancy, including lead poisoning and fetal alcohol syndrome.

FAMILY HISTORY

The fact that learning disabilities tend to run in families indicates that there may be a genetic link. For example, children who lack some of the skills needed for reading, such as hearing the separate sounds (phonemes) of words, are likely to have a parent with a related problem. However, a parent's learning disability may take a slightly different form in the child. A parent who has a writing disorder, for example, may have a child with a mathematics disorder. For this reason, it seems unlikely that specific learning disorders are inherited directly. What is inherited may be a subtle brain dysfunction that can in turn lead to a learning problem.

In addition to genetic inheritance, there may be an alternative explanation for why learning disorders run in families. Some learning difficulties may actually stem from the family environment. For example, parents who have expressive language disorders might talk less to their children, or the language they use may be distorted. In such cases, the child lacks a good model for acquiring language and therefore may develop symptoms of a learning disorder (Neuwirth, 1993).

MEDICAL CONDITIONS

Whereas family influences have been studied since the early 1900s, the effects of medical complications have received significant attention

OVERCOMING A LEARNING DISORDER: TOM CRUISE

Thomas Cruise Mapother never liked school as a child. Early in his school years, he was labeled a slow learner, because of his difficulties with reading, spelling, and writing. Yet because his family moved around so frequently, he never stayed in one school system long enough to benefit from an individualized or specialized education program for his learning disorder. Teachers, seeing that he was intelligent, often just pushed him through the curriculum and passed him despite his obvious struggles. Despite his mother's attempts to make school at least somewhat helpful, Tom's academic career was never enjoyable. "I would come home crying . . . because of the misery of not being able to do as well in school as I knew I should be able to," he has said.

Fortunately, Tom found an outlet for his creativity and intelligence in acting. After participating in a high school play convinced him he wanted to act, he moved to New York to take acting lessons and audition for parts in movies and television commercials. In auditions, Tom would try to work around his dyslexia by reading the first few lines of his script, then ad-libbing in the direction the scene seemed to go. Thanks to his creative intensity, this unusual technique paid off, landing Tom in bigger and better roles as his career went on. After several false starts, Tom Cruise landed a series of small movie roles, and finally the lead in *Risky Business*, which brought him to the media's attention and into the "role" of celebrity.

In 1985, Tom Cruise was presented with an award for Outstanding Learning Disabled Achievement in a ceremony at the White House. The six films he had played parts in at that time—and blockbuster hits like *Top Gun*, *Mission: Impossible*, and *Jerry Maguire* since then—proved without a doubt that Tom's dyslexia was not a barrier to his success.

only over the last few decades. A number of studies indicate that drugs taken by the mother pass directly to the fetus. Such research reveals that a mother's use of cigarettes, alcohol, or other drugs during pregnancy may damage the unborn child.

Mothers who smoke during pregnancy are more likely to bear smaller babies. And small newborns, usually those weighing less than five pounds, tend to be at risk for a variety of problems, including learning disorders.

A mother's consumption of alcohol also endangers the fetus's developing brain, as it appears to distort the developing neurons. Mothers who drink heavily during pregnancy are at higher risk for delivering a baby with fetal alcohol syndrome, a condition that can lead to low birth weight, intellectual impairment, hyperactivity, and certain physical defects. Even light alcohol use during pregnancy can influence the child's development and lead to problems with learning, attention, memory, or problem solving.

The use of other drugs, such as cocaine—especially in the smokable form known as crack—also seems to affect the normal development of brain receptors. These brain cell parts help to transmit incoming signals from our skin, eyes, and ears and help to regulate our physical response to our environment. Because children with certain learning disorders have difficulty understanding speech sounds or letters, some researchers believe that learning disabilities, as well as ADHD, may be related to faulty receptors (Neuwirth, 1993).

OTHER POSSIBLE COMPLICATIONS

In some cases, the mother's immune system reacts to the fetus and attacks it as if it were an infection. This type of disruption during pregnancy seems to cause newly formed brain cells to settle in the wrong part of the brain. Another possible complication is that during delivery, the umbilical cord can become twisted and temporarily cut off oxygen to the fetus. This, too, can impair brain functions and lead to learning disorders. Finally, poisons in the child's environment, such as the toxic dust from lead-based paint, can result in severe impairments. As new brain cells continue to be produced for a year or so after the child is born, such poisons can disrupt cell development and lead to inattention, disruptive behavior, and other problems later on (Neuwirth, 1993).

Despite all of these potential contributors to learning disorder, the APA points out that the severity of symptoms and duration of the disorder can be lessened or exacerbated by learning and experience. In fact, as children mature, educational and environmental factors should ultimately interact to help them overcome their difficulties. Many people with learning disorders achieve goals in life well beyond what was initially expected of them. And given the great number of famous and not-so-famous individuals who have learned to master a learning disorder, it appears that those struggling with such obstacles have significantly greater potential and special talents than is currently understood (Popper and Steingard, 1994).

READING DISORDER

Given the diversity of possible causes, it is generally accepted that reading disorder is not a one-dimensional condition and that a variety of factors can affect the same individual. Moreover, the combination of factors that leads to dyslexia affects each individual differently. Rather than try to define the causes of reading disorder, it is better to understand the various neurological, family, medical, and cultural contributors described as risk factors. Maternal smoking, low birth weight, and birth mishaps, especially, may contribute to the development of dyslexia. Each one of these factors, alone or in combination, can increase the severity of a reading disorder.

Although learning to read can be compromised in a variety of ways, reading disorder is a neurological disease that can be seen even in the presence of normal intelligence, education, motivation, and emotional control. Common dyslexia is characterized by slow reading speed, impaired comprehension, word omissions and distortions, and letter reversals, despite normal to high IQ. For reading skills to develop in the normal way, certain functions must be intact. Eye control to prevent slipping off letters or lines, spatial orientation enabling letters and words to be read from the left, and the ability to retain a memory of letter forms, sequence words, grasp the structural sense of a sentence, and comprehend what is read all require intact eye and brain functions.

In addition to these functions, there is a simultaneous use of perception in shape discrimination, spacing and timing, sight and sound processing, linguistic sound processing, and understanding of grammar and meaning. Attention, motivation, and effort must be intact. Also necessary are "reading readiness" skills, including the ability to take instruction and to avoid disrupting other individuals in the classroom. Generally, reading ability, especially verbal coding and sequencing, depends on a person's IQ. A reading disorder might result from neurological or medical problems affecting any of these functions.

As has been mentioned, dyslexia—like most learning disorders—runs in families. Psychiatric histories show an overrepresentation of reading disorder in the siblings and parents of individuals with dyslexia.

A young boy takes an eye test. Poor eyesight is not the same as a reading disorder, but can cause many of the same problems for a child who cannot clearly see what he or she must read or write.

However, given proper diagnosis and treatment, family members can also work together to alleviate the difficulties associated with reading disorder. In fact, family support is crucial to overcoming any learning disorder. The future of a person dealing with dyslexia can also be greatly influenced by educational opportunities, individual personality, and ambition.

It is important to note that reading disorders are distinct from the problem of slow reading. Individuals with reading disorder, for example, usually exhibit an average or above-average IQ, whereas those with a simple slowness in acquiring reading skills often have a lower level of intelligence compared with their peers (Popper and Steingard, 1994). Difficulty in reading can also result from mental retardation, brain damage, psychiatric disturbance (especially influences on attention and anxiety) and hearing and vision problems. These conditions are not reading disorders.

MATHEMATICS DISORDER

Arithmetic involves recognizing numbers and symbols, memorizing facts such as the multiplication table, aligning numbers, and understanding abstract concepts like place value and fractions. Any of these may be difficult for children with developmental arithmetic disorders. Problems with numbers or basic concepts are likely to show up early. Disabilities that appear in the later grades are more often tied to problems in reasoning (Neuwirth, 1993).

The cause or origin of mathematics disorder is not completely understood or well defined. Damage to the language-dominant hemisphere of the brain, as seen in reading disorder, is not as apparent in this condition. Although the neurological causes are not so clear, several other possible contributors have been suggested. Slow development of mathematical abilities is assumed to be affected by neurological and genetic factors as well as by psychological and socioeconomic conditions. Learning experiences also weigh heavily in reducing or increasing the difficulties associated with mathematics disorder. Learning mathematical skills successfully depends greatly on IQ and classroom training. However, mathematics disorder is diagnosed for individuals who have a specific neurological or psychiatric abnormality; it does not apply to those who are merely slow learners or who have poor educational opportunities.

DISORDER OF WRITTEN EXPRESSION

Writing, too, involves several brain areas and functions. Problems with written expression may result from underlying difficulties with hand-and-pencil control, fine motor and visual motor function, attention, memory, concept formation, organization (prioritizing and flow), and expressive language function. The brain networks for vocabulary, grammar, hand movement, and memory must all be in good working order. A developmental writing disorder may therefore result from problems in any of these areas.

A person with disorder of written expression may not be able to distinguish the sequence of sounds in a word and, therefore, will have problems with spelling. Another person with the disorder might be unable to compose complete, grammatical sentences (Neuwirth, 1993). Ultimately, as with other learning disabilities, disorder of written expression is presumed to result from neurological characteristics that can be changed for the better by one's individual personality and positive experiences both at home and at school.

A teacher explains the lesson to a puzzled boy. With therapy and help from understanding parents and teachers, children can overcome their learning disorders.

6

TREATMENT OF
LEARNING DISORDERS

Traditionally, learning disorders were considered to be a school problem because that is where the symptoms were most evident. But over time, it has become clear that these disorders affect all aspects of a person's life. The difficulties experienced by an individual with a learning disorder may interfere with his or her social behavior and the development of healthy peer relationships. And these difficulties have an impact not only on the individual but also on the functioning of his or her family as a whole.

To treat individuals with learning disorders successfully, a therapist must look at as many potential causes as possible. Initially, many students with learning disorders are referred to therapy for help because of their behavioral problems or difficulty with anxiety or depression. But before a person with such problems can be evaluated for treatment, it must be determined whether emotional, social, or family difficulties are the source of academic problems or, conversely, whether struggles with academic subjects result in these behavioral problems (Silver, 1995).

Once such preliminary concerns are resolved, a number of treatment options can be considered. In fact, therapy usually takes many forms. The special education and related services needed to address the learning disorder must be established. The student's teachers must be informed immediately and asked to provide the necessary accommodations. The child with the disorder and his or her family also need to understand the neurological problems underlying the learning disorder. All need to take a fresh look at how these disabilities affect every aspect of the youngster's life.

A program of treatment that considers school, family, and peer relationships and how each is affected by the child's learning disorder must be devel-

Most learning disorders are evident by the end of first grade, when children should have a basic understanding of reading, writing, and math skills. The earlier a disorder is detected, the more easily it can be treated.

oped. If such a program is created, the child or adolescent can be successful both in and outside school. Without this comprehensive approach, however, the outcome could be academic failure, serious emotional difficulties, family dysfunction, and social problems (Silver, 1995).

RECOGNIZING THE SYMPTOMS

If a child's problematic behavior is not recognized and evaluated early as a possible learning disorder, he or she may suffer needlessly. The following case illustrates the importance of timely and appropriate assessment.

■   ■   ■

Billy started first grade and did not do well. He couldn't master the early skills of reading and writing, so his school system made him repeat the year. Unfortunately, Billy didn't make much progress during his second year of first grade, either. However, because of his age, he was promoted to second grade. Despite his efforts to keep up, he fell further and further behind. By the time Billy entered third grade, he was overwhelmed and unable to do the work in class or at home. He knew that he was a year older than the other students, and this made him feel frustrated and dumb. Soon, he began to clown around in class and get into fights with the other students.

Over the course of Billy's third-grade year, his teacher grew increasingly impatient with his lack of progress. He was disrupting the class and preventing her from teaching the other children. Rather than exploring possible underlying causes, the teacher took her frustration out on Billy's parents. She phoned them repeatedly, reporting, "Billy is not completing his schoolwork." "His homework is incorrect." "He is teasing and fighting with the other children." Her message was clear: "Do something. Fix your kid." At home, Billy's parents were just as confused and frustrated as the teacher. They had begun to disagree, with one parent thinking that the best way to help Billy was to be firm and strict, while the other preferred a more understanding and permissive approach.

Eventually, the school principal called in the parents, informing them that Billy was not making academic progress. The principal believed Billy was emotionally disturbed as a result of his parents' marital problems. The possibility of a learning disorder was not even acknowledged. Instead, the principal merely encouraged the parents to see a mental health professional (Silver, 1995).

■　　　　■　　　　■

This vignette highlights the importance of both school staff and family members in recognizing the presence of a learning disorder in a child. It also touches on the impact the disorder can have on an entire family. Ideally, the next step for Billy would involve meeting with a family therapist who would be more likely to uncover the root of his behavioral problems and his parents' difficulties. Once the cause (or causes) of the problems is addressed, behavioral problems and family conflicts can, hopefully, be resolved (Silver, 1995).

In addition to recognizing a disorder, it is important to understand that learning disorders are life disabilities. A child with a learning disorder will become an adolescent with a learning disorder and eventually an adult with a learning disorder. These neurologically based disorders

One of the most important parts of treatment for learning-disabled children is finding outlets for expression in which they can feel confident in their abilities and intelligence.

do not go away. And they are often pervasive. In other words, the same problems that interfere with reading, writing, or doing mathematics may interfere with playing baseball or basketball, jumping rope, playing hopscotch, cutting up food, dressing oneself, making small talk, and many other life skills (Silver, 1995).

Learning disabilities affect peer interactions and play, family interactions and expectations, and tasks required during such non-school activities as Boy or Girl Scouts, Sunday school, and camp. In Billy's case, his clowning around in the classroom and provocation of peers largely reflected his low self-esteem and subsequent feelings of frustration and failure. In other situations, parents might get angry at their child for not listening to them, when, in fact, the child may actually be having trouble understanding their question or statement because of a limited ability to process what he or she hears.

TYPES OF THERAPY

Before specific behavioral problems can be addressed, the child and family should understand what causes a learning disorder. With a better understanding of the disorder, the family can then devise new, constructive ways to work with the youngster. To deal with any resulting stress in their marriage, parents may also benefit from couples therapy. Individual therapy can help those individuals with more severe learning difficulties. At the same time, many youngsters may require a special focus on their social skills (Silver, 1995).

THE FIRST STEP: EDUCATION

A child or adolescent with a learning disorder has had the same brain all of his or her life, so these individuals do not know that they are different. They know they try as hard as everyone else, yet they do not succeed. They try to be good, yet parents and teachers seem to be disappointed in them or angry with them. Thus, once the diagnosis is established, it is critical that someone explain to these individuals what the problems are, focusing not only on the areas of learning difficulties but also on the areas of learning strengths.

Parents must also understand this information so that they can develop a better understanding of their child. A therapist can help the individual and the family members identify problem areas and discuss how these areas have affected family members, friendships, and activities.

With proper counseling, the youngster with a learning disorder can begin to look at himself or herself in different, more positive ways. Parents also can be coached on ways to understand their child and to adjust their responses and behavior in an effort to stimulate the child's self-confidence. Siblings might gain a new understanding of the problems in the family as well.

If the behavioral problems are not serious, family education may be all that is needed. It may be that once the academic issues are addressed and the family begins to change, the behavioral problems disappear and no further help is necessary. If more counseling is needed, this initial step helps to clarify which type of therapy would be most appropriate (Silver, 1995).

FAMILY THERAPY

The next logical step is often family counseling, in which parents are taught how to use their knowledge of their child's strengths and weaknesses to change old family habits. Adjustment might include choosing appropriate chores, encouraging certain activities and sports, and addressing stress issues within the family. Often, once taught the necessary knowledge about their child and possible methods for working with his or her difficulties, families can move ahead and creatively work out their own problems.

Each member of the family must develop a better understanding of the family member with a learning disorder. Parents need to have a clearer picture of their child's specific strengths and weaknesses. Then, once they've become more sensitive to behavior that is largely caused by the disorder, they can prepare ways for helping their son or daughter succeed both within and outside of the family.

At home, the youngster can be responsible for certain household chores. If he or she has visual motor and fine motor disabilities, for example, loading or unloading the dishwasher might be difficult. However, he or she could walk the dog, take out the trash, or bring in the newspaper. Each of these tasks requires very little eye-hand coordination or fine motor skills. Parents learn to build on strengths to select appropriate chores rather than to assign tasks that might be difficult or not to assign chores at all. In this way, they spare themselves and their child needless frustration.

The same approach can be used in selecting clubs, activities, and sports for the child. Each sport requires different strengths. If the individual has visual perception, visual motor, and fine motor disabilities, he or she might have difficulty with sports that require quick eye-hand coordination, such as baseball or basketball. On the other hand, sports that require more gross motor abilities with minimal need for quick eye-hand coordination, including swimming, soccer, bowling, horseback riding, sailing, canoeing, and certain field and track events, would be more enjoyable and thus would build the child's confidence. If the child has difficulty with listening skills, the parents should also make sure the coach is aware of their child's difficulties and that he or she may need to repeat instructions to the child individually (Silver, 1995).

Psychological testing, such as the mirror test shown here, and counseling can help to determine what kind of aid a student needs and how best to teach the student to function in the classroom.

INDIVIDUAL THERAPY

For some youngsters, a learning disorder is accompanied by emotional or behavioral problems that often result in frustration and failure in school or with peers and the family. These individuals need help understanding themselves and learning better methods of handling stress and conflict. For others, initial stress might have been caused by the learning disability, but the resulting conflicts and patterns of defense have become so established that relieving the stress in school will not be enough. Both types of youngsters benefit from individual psychotherapy.

In many cases, children with learning disorders have so deeply internalized feelings of low self-worth that more intense therapy might be needed to help them improve their self-image. Youngsters with learning disorder need to understand that they are not "dumb"—they have a

Sports that require less quick hand-eye coordination and more gross motor skills, such as soccer, can be good activities for children with learning disorders.

learning disability, which means they have many strengths and also weaknesses. So they must learn to embrace the former and manage the latter to move beyond their disabilities and achieve higher goals. Once the child becomes confident with this newly gained knowledge of self, he or she can rethink and overcome painful memories of past experiences. In the process, the youngster inevitably develops a more positive self-image and higher self-esteem (Silver, 1995).

COUPLES THERAPY

In addition to family and individual counseling, couples therapy for the parents might be necessary. Couples therapy can help the parents understand the impact their child's previously unrecognized and untreated learning disorder has had on them as parents and as a couple.

Because studies suggest that there is an inherited, familial pattern in approximately 40 percent of individuals with a learning disability, it is important to explore the possibility that one of the parents has the same difficulty. Such awareness may help explain a history of past difficulties and will help the parent improve his or her parenting skills.

Parents also must use their new understanding of their child to rethink the way they view him or her. Family and couples therapy can help them become more aware of the behavior typically associated with learning disorders, which in turn enables parents to learn new strategies for helping the child within the family as well as outside of the home. Often through this process, the stress experienced between the parents decreases (Silver, 1995).

SOCIAL SKILLS THERAPY

Youngsters with learning disorders often have problems relating to their peers. For many, it is a challenge to read social cues or learn social skills. It is not known why these problems commonly accompany learning disabilities. Those with the disorder may have difficulty interpreting body language or tone of voice and may act inappropriately in social situations. In such cases, social skills training can be helpful, especially since early problems with social interaction can lead to later difficulties in adolescence and adulthood.

Social skills therapy focuses on changing specific behavioral patterns and thought processes into more competent, positive social behavior. Treatment is directed toward the underlying factors that are linked to positive peer acceptance. Helping individuals improve social skills typically involves three kinds of skill development: accurate interpretation of social situations, effective use of social behaviors in interactions with others, and evaluation of one's own performance and the ability to adjust depending on the situation. Role-playing, in which the child rehearses skills with a therapist in a variety of situations, provides reinforcement and corrective feedback. Encouraged by the role-playing, the child can then practice his or her new skills in more natural settings, like the classroom (Silver, 1995).

READING DISORDER

It has been noted throughout this volume that developmental reading disorder cannot be cured. Even with appropriate educational arrangements, youngsters with this disorder learn to read and spell at a slower rate than do normally developing individuals. But the student with developmental reading disorder can learn to compensate and live a well-adjusted, productive life, both personally and professionally.

OVERCOMING DYSLEXIA: CHARLES SCHWAB

C harles Schwab, a pioneer in the investing world, was determined that nothing, not even dyslexia, would keep him from becoming a success. Today, Charles Schwab & Co. is the largest discount broker in the country, made prosperous by business practices that Schwab implemented during the 1970s.

Charles Schwab was born in Sacremento, California, in 1937. His father, a small-town lawyer, taught him the value of money and the importance of spending it prudently. Listening to his father's stories of the Great Depression motivated Charles to work hard to achieve his goal of financial security.

Although his dyslexia made reading and learning difficult, Charles learned to work with the skills that he already had in order to build new ones, and in this way overcame the obstacles that his learning disorder presented. He read classic books such as *Moby Dick* and *Ivanhoe* in an easy-to-understand comic book format, and battled a common side effect of learning disorders, low self-esteem, by making friends and honing his talent for investment and finance. His first business venture, at age 8, was picking walnuts and selling 100-pound bags for $5 each. At age 13 he began reading stock tables; a few years later, he had purchased his first shares of stock—100 shares valued at $1 each. In 1959, he earned a bachelor's degree in economics from Stanford University, one of the finest universities in the country. A few years later, he earned an M.B.A. from Stanford's Graduate School of Business.

Schwab founded his brokerage firm in California in 1971 with a $100,000 loan. A few years later, he introduced the business practices that would make him a billionaire. He turned his brokerage firm into a "discount broker"—a no-frills style of buying and selling stocks that made personal investing easier and less expensive for the average consumer. In 1985 the man who had difficulty reading as a child became an author: he published his investment philosophy in the book *How to Be Your Own Stockbroker* (MacMillan).

Today, in addition to his business and roles as a member of the Stanford University Board of Trustees and as treasurer of the National Park Foundation, Schwab volunteers his time as the chairman of Parent's Educational Resource Center in San Mateo, California. This nonprofit organization helps parents of children with learning disabilities get the extra support and acquire the skills they need to help their children learn.

To assess whether a person does in fact have a learning disorder, as well as to determine how severe it might be, clinicians use a variety of tests. Measurement of hearing and vision are used to rule out the possibility of sensory deficits, while IQ tests indicate whether lower intelligence, which, as we know, is different from a reading disorder, is the actual problem. Neurological and psychiatric assessments can reveal the influence of other conditions, such as disruptive behavior disorders like attention-deficit/hyperactivity or conduct disorders, and communication disorders. Once these other possible complications have been explored, specific tests that rate reading speed, reading comprehension, and spelling can be applied.

Direct, one-on-one instruction in reading, spelling, and writing is considered the essential academic treatment for a student with a reading disorder. These efforts are provided by a person trained to use appropriate remedial methods that emphasize letter-sound association drills. This specialized instruction challenges students to learn by using a number of senses. For example, children see a letter and hear its name and sound; they then trace the letter, saying its name and sound; and finally they write the letter, repeating its name and sound. Sounds and letters are then blended to form words. Reading, spelling, and writing are taught simultaneously, and children are given plenty of lessons to practice what they've learned. These lessons are supplemented by speech training and study skills instructions (McDermott and Weller, 1995).

To alleviate further the stress associated with writing, a student also might be encouraged to use a word processor for assignments. As individuals with reading disorders often require more time for understanding questions and solving problems, they might also be permitted to take "time-extended" tests. Individual tutoring is often helpful, too. Studying can be facilitated by the use of self-paced programmed texts or computerized self-instruction.

At home, parents can help by reading to their children, just as General George Patton's family (see Chapter 1) did for him. This practice enhances children's appreciation of reading and gives them access to knowledge normally obtainable only by reading for themselves. Ultimately, the overall goals of treatment are to emphasize success, develop pride, foster enjoyment of mastering a skill, and enhance general learning by promoting interests in new situations and new experiences (McDermott and Weller, 1995).

MATHEMATICS DISORDER

Successful treatment of mathematics disorder requires a close examination of the underlying difficulty that the child is having with math. While some students may have problems understanding the basic concepts of arithmetic and as a result cannot make calculations, others may have difficulties with the structured process of learning arithmetic. Because math achievement is highly dependent on the quality of instruction offered to students, it must first be determined whether classroom problems are simply a result of poor instruction in basic concepts. For remedial efforts to be effective, they must correctly address the student's problem area.

Before children learn arithmetic in school, they have an informal knowledge of numbers and have developed strategies based on their own experience (Silver, 1995). Relying on this informal knowledge, children often develop their own method of counting. When they are introduced to math education in school, they may experience some difficulties, because formal teaching depends on an understanding and application of formulas that are not intuitively clear. For example, young children need to understand the key concept that our numerical system is based on the number 10.

Some children or adolescents with mathematics disorder have trouble learning and using number words (such as "multiplication" or "integer") and concepts (like addition or decimal conversions); they also may write numbers incorrectly, or misalign them when performing computations. For example, the student may have problems lining up numbers in columns of "ones," "tens," "hundreds," etc. Where the correct formula would be

$$\begin{array}{r} 63 \\ +\ 2 \\ \hline 65 \end{array}$$

The student with mathematics disorder may consistently write

$$\begin{array}{r} 63 \\ +2\ \\ \hline 83 \end{array}$$

Others experience difficulties in understanding basic numeric concepts or in applying arithmetic skills when solving everyday problems.

Because traditional mathematics instruction emphasizes obtaining

One-on-one therapy, tailored to the student's particular problems, seems to be the best way to help the student overcome a learning disorder and be successful.

the right answer over problem solving, children may become anxious about attempting to perform calculations, or feel that they are "stupid." For some, pressure for speedy answers to math problems can lead them to guess at questions impulsively, rather than trying to calculate the correct answer. Adding to the problem, students who have difficulty memorizing may be criticized for trying to compensate by using their fingers to count, marking down intermediate calculations, and other methods.

Therapists and teachers can provide some useful tools and techniques to help students overcome their difficulties with arithmetic. Some may find their problems reduced or eliminated if they are permitted to use a calculator, whereas others may benefit most from individual

TWO PARENTS' POINTS OF VIEW

MRS. S.: Stevie's difficulties began when he was learning to read. I guess he would be called a slow learner. He was always a bit on the active side but not hyperactive. He has always felt different from the other kids. He's in seventh grade now and it's getting even harder. Kids don't want to feel different, especially in adolescence.

I am a divorced single parent. That's exacerbated Stevie's problems. There are so many things I feel guilty about. Divorce breeds insecurity and guilt on both sides. His father is much more of a disciplinarian and finger pointer. It's hard on a kid.

We had Stevie tested at the end of second grade. The report was not terribly specific. They said his IQ was average to above average. They stressed that it would be important for him to go to a structured school and for us to be very consistent with him.

They also suggested the possible use of Ritalin because of his active nature. We had him tested again at another hospital and they were even more insistent about trying Ritalin.

I didn't want Stevie to be on a drug. I want my son to learn to control his activity himself. I feared the drug would inhibit his growth. So I just never considered it strongly. His activity level has decreased since he's gotten older. Socially, he's a very adept child. He's also lucky because he's good at sports. But he really doesn't feel confident about his ability no matter what I tell him. Inside, he doesn't believe he's capable if he's had to get all this help. I tell him you just have to work on it.

MRS. D.: Chris was always a sweet kid—considerate. Of all my children, he gave me the least trouble. I returned to work when he was in the second grade. Shortly after that, we began to notice that he was having trouble. Spelling was difficult for him; math and reading were not easy either. On my nights off, I would sit with Chris and try to help him with his homework. It was a frustrating experience. By the end of the evening, I would ask him a question, but instead of answering me he would just say, "I don't know." This would go on for hours. How do you spell this? "I don't know." What is 2 times 4? "I don't know." What is this word? "I don't know!"

His difficulties with math, I thought, were understandable. I had never been very good with numbers, though my husband is. Our two other children grasped it easily, but Chris always struggled with it. I thought it must have been something he inherited from me—this math "dumbness." The rest, though, I began to think was just Chris's way of getting even with me for leaving him each afternoon to go to work. Even though he had an older brother and sister and his father usually came home two hours after school got out, I thought that my working had somehow interfered with Chris's schooling—maybe he wasn't getting enough help at home, maybe he just wasn't trying anymore.

Sometimes when I tried to help him, I would end up screaming, "You're not trying!" and poor Chris would start crying and scream, "I am! I'm just dumb!" and throw his book on the floor and run out.

At the end of that year, the parochial school Chris attended decided to leave him back. I was crushed, and so was Chris. Thank God, Chris's teacher finally spoke up. She told me she thought Chris was very bright—that perhaps he just had a learning disability. I didn't really know that much about learning disabilities, but my husband and I took Chris to be evaluated, and, sure enough, that's what it turned out to be.

In order to get the help he needed, we transferred Chris to a public school. There he worked with other children in a resource room to complete his homework and work out any tough problems. Chris had some trouble learning as fast as the other kids in a normal setting. Fortunately, he also had another wonderful teacher who was willing to stay after school with him and come in early to help with the topics they were covering in class.

During high school, Chris attended vocational classes in electricity along with his regular classwork. He soon found that he was really good at electric work—he was bringing home straight A's. Today, Chris is training to be an electrician. He has outgrown his learning disability and is never frustrated by things anymore. His life is really on track.

Source: Jean McBee Knox, Learning Disabilities *(New York: Chelsea House Publishers, 1989): pp. 36-37.*

tutoring. Self-paced programmed texts or computerized self-instruction software may also be helpful (Silver, 1995). In a programmed text, instruction is given in "levels," and students must master each level before moving on to the next, ensuring that all information is understood rather than simply moving on after a certain amount of time. With self-paced programmed textbooks, as in computerized self-instruction, students can take as much time as they need to grasp each concept.

Treatment for mathematics disorder also involves dealing with the related problems of repeated failure—anxiety, withdrawal, and feelings of hopelessness—that are commonly seen in children with a learning disability.

DISORDER OF WRITTEN EXPRESSION

Traditionally, little emphasis has been placed on writing in the early school grades. Much more time has been spent on reading instruction. This approach is justified by the observation that receptive language skills in babies emerge before spoken words. Because babies can understand before they can speak, it has been assumed that school-age children should read before they write. Until reading skills are well established, writing is usually assigned a minor role in instruction. Both reading and writing require the ability to attach the correct sounds (phonemes) to the correct symbols (graphemes). Reading requires the ability to decode letters into sounds and blend these sounds into words. Writing requires the ability to then reapply the language or sounds in the brain back into graphic symbols. Thus, reading and writing problems are frequently seen together (Silver, 1995).

Poor spelling might be the first indication of a writing disorder. By the third or fourth grade, additional writing problems often become apparent. Children with a writing disorder tend to exhibit grammatical and punctuation errors at the sentence level. Paragraphs may be poorly organized. In later grades, taking notes is usually difficult for the student, as it is nearly impossible for those with a writing disorder to analyze a rapidly paced lecture and to write at the same time (Silver, 1995).

Formal methods for assessment and measurement of expressive writing have not been developed, so clinicians typically rely on samples of copied, dictated, and spontaneous writing (Popper and Steingard, 1994). Treatment for a writing disorder might involve a skills approach or a holistic approach. Skills programs, often used with younger children, focus on letter-sound associations and often emphasize reading as well as spelling. For example, children might be asked to listen carefully for sounds in words and then to represent these sounds with written letters, saying each letter aloud as it is written (Silver, 1995).

The holistic approach to writing begins with the student's ideas. It involves a series of highly structured steps for narrowing ideas to one topic, writing a first draft, reading it aloud to an audience of peers, and then refining organization and language. The final step involves working on the mechanics of organizing the paper into a draft for peers to read (Silver, 1995).

Most efforts combine these two approaches. Children with a writing disorder need direct, sequential instruction in letter-sound associations and in spelling rules, as well as in sentence construction and the mechanics of punctuation and capitalization. But even with intensive special instruction, writing for these students requires an enormous effort. Quite often, accommodations are needed throughout the individual's education. And because this disorder cannot be cured but can only be compensated for, such adaptive methods are typically used well into adulthood (Silver, 1995).

APPENDIX

FOR MORE INFORMATION

Parents of children and adolescents with psychiatric disorders, together with mental health professionals and teachers, have established national organizations that provide education and support for parents, as well as advocacy services and research facilities. Many of these national groups also have local chapters that tend to focus on a particular disorder and serve as a powerful adjunct to direct clinical services.

American Academy of Child and Adolescent Psychiatry (AACAP)
3615 Wisconsin Ave., NW
Washington, DC 20016-3007
(202) 966-7300
http://www.aacap.org/

American Speech-Language-Hearing Association (ASHA)
10801 Rockville Pike
Rockville, MD 20852
(301) 897-5700
http://www.asha.org/

Association on Higher Education and Disability (AHEAD)
P.O. Box 21192
Columbus, OH 43221-0192
(614) 488-4972
http://www.ahead.org/

Canadian Mental Health Association (CMHA)
970 Lawrence Ave. West
Suite 205
Toronto, Ontario M6A 3B6
Canada
(416) 789-7957
http://www.icomm.ca/cmhacan/

Council for Exceptional Children, Eric Clearinghouse on Disabilities & Gifted Children
1920 Association Dr.
Reston, VA 22091
(800) 328-0272
http://www.cec.sped.org/ericec.htm

Council for Learning Disabilities
P.O. Box 40303
Overland Park, KS 66204
(913) 492-8755
http://www1.winthrop.edu/cld/

Gow School
Emery Rd.
South Wales, NY 14139
(716) 652-3450, (800) 724-0138
http://www.gow.org/

The International Dyslexia Association
8600 Lasalle Rd.
Chester Building, Suite 382
Baltimore, MD 21286
(410) 296-0232, (800) 222-3123
http://www.interdys.org/

Kennedy Krieger Institute
707 North Broadway
Baltimore, MD 21205
(888) 554-2080
http://www.kennedykrieger.org/

Learning Disabilities Association of America (LDAA)
4156 Library Rd.
Pittsburgh, PA 15234
(412) 341-1515, (412) 341-8077
http://www.ldnatl.org/

Learning Disabilities Association of Canada (LDAC)
323 Chapel St.
Suite 200
Ottawa, Ontario K1N 7Z2
Canada
(613) 238-5721
http://educ.queensu.ca/~lda

National Alliance for the Mentally Ill Child and Adolescent Network (NAMI-CAN)
200 North Glebe Rd.
Suite 1015
Arlington, VA 22203-3754
(800) 950-NAMI
http://www.nami.org

National Center for Learning Disabilities
381 Park Ave. South
Suite 1420
New York, NY 10016
(212) 545-7510
http://www.ncld.org/

National Information Center for Children and Youth with Disabilities (NICHCY)
P.O. Box 1492
Washington, DC 20013
(800) 695-0285
http://www.nichcy.org/

NAWA (an alternative to traditional education)
17351 Trinity Mountain Rd.
French Gulch, CA 96033
(800) 358-NAWA
http://www.internet-connect.com/nawa/

Parents & Educators Resource Center
1660 South Amphlett Boulevard
Suite 200
San Mateo, CA 94402-2508
(650) 655-2410
http://www.perc-schwabfdn.org/

APPENDIX

ENTITLEMENTS OF THE EDUCATION FOR ALL HANDICAPPED CHILDREN ACT AND ITS LATER REVISION, INDIVIDUALS WITH DISABILITIES EDUCATION ACT (IDEA)

❶ A free public education is guaranteed for all individuals between the ages of 3 and 21.

❷ Each person is guaranteed an "individualized education program," or IEP. The IEP must be written, must be jointly developed by the school, teacher, and parent, and must include an analysis of the student's present achievement level, difficulties, and goals. Specific services that are to be provided must be identified. Specific ways of assessing progress must be noted.

❸ Children with disabilities and without disabilities must be educated together to the fullest extent that is appropriate. In other words, students with disabilities must be educated in the "least restrictive environment" that will allow for the necessary services. The level of services need not mean that education is provided in the regular classroom. For some students the least restrictive environment might be the most restrictive environment.

❹ Tests and other evaluation materials used must be prepared and administered in such a way as not to be racially or culturally discriminatory. They must be presented, when needed, in the child's native language.

❺ These rights and guarantees apply to children in private as well as in public schools. That is, students in private schools are entitled to receive the same services from the public school as students in the public school.

Under law, there are procedural safeguards. Parents have the right to examine any records that bear on the identification of their child as being disabled, on the defined nature and severity of the disability, and on the educational setting proposed for placement. Schools must provide written notice before changing a child's placement. If a parent or guardian objects to a school's decision, there must be a process in place by which complaints can be registered. This process must include an opportunity for an impartial hearing that offers parents rights similar to those involved in court (i.e., the right to be advised by counsel, to present evidence, to cross-examine witnesses, etc.). All final decisions must be in writing.

Source: *Treatment of Psychiatric Disorders*, 2nd ed.

FAMOUS PEOPLE WITH LEARNING DISORDERS

Although not all of these famous people have been officially diagnosed, they have exhibited many of the signs of learning disorders. The point of this list, which was compiled by the Davis Research Foundation, is to demonstrate that learning disorders can be overcome.

Actors
Cher
Tom Cruise
Danny Glover
Whoopi Goldberg
Anthony Hopkins
Henry Winkler

Artists
Walt Disney
Pablo Picasso
August Rodin
Leonardo da Vinci

Athletes
Bruce Jenner
Greg Louganis
Jackie Stewart

Entrepreneur
Steve Jobs

Inventors/Scientists
Alexander Graham Bell
Thomas Edison
Albert Einstein

Mathematicians
John Von Neumann
Sir Isaac Newton

Military/Political Leaders
George Bush
Winston Churchill
Lyndon Johnson
George Patton
Nelson Rockefeller
Woodrow Wilson

Writers/Poets
Hans Christian Anderson
Agatha Christie
John Irvine
William Butler Yeats

APPENDIX

SOURCES CITED

Baker, E. T. "Meta-analytic evidence for non-inclusive educational practices: Does educational research support current practice for special-needs students?" (Ph.D. dissertation, Temple University, 1994).

Baker, E. T., M. C. Wang, and H. J. Walberg. "The effects of inclusion on learning." *Educational Leadership* 42, no. 4 (April 1995).

Carlberg, C., and K. Kavale. "The efficacy of special versus regular class placement for exceptional children: A meta-analysis." *Journal of Special Education* 14 (1980).

Cook, E. H., Jr., and B. L. Leventhal. "Neuropsychiatric Disorders." *Textbook of Neuropsychiatry*, 2nd edition. Washington D.C.: American Psychiatric Press, 1992.

Coordinated Campaign for Learning Disabilities (CCLD). [On-line] Available: www.ldonline.org/ccld.

Davis, R. "Dyslexia, the Gift." Davis Dyslexia Association International, 1997. Available at: www.dyslexia.com.

D'Este, Carlo. *Patton: A Genius for War*. New York: HarperCollins, 1995.

Feldman, E., et al. "Adult Familial Dyslexia: A Retrospective Developmental and Psychosocial Profile." *Journal of Neuropsychiatry and Clinical Neurosciences* 5, no. 2 (Summer 1993).

Fras, Ivan. "Book Forum." *American Journal of Psychiatry* 153, no. 12 (December 1996).

Heller, K., W. Holtzman, and S. Messick. *Placing Children in Special Education: A Strategy for Equity*. Washington, D.C.: National Academy of Science Press, 1982.

Lyon, G. Reid. "Neuroimaging: Understanding How the Brain Works." *Journal of Child Neurology* 10, no. 1 (January 1995). Available at: www.ldonline.org/ccld.

———. "Towards a Definition of Dyslexia." *Annals of Dyslexia* 45 (1995).

Available at : www.ldonline.org/ccld.

McDermott, J. F., Jr., and E. B. Weller. "Disorders Usually First Diagnosed in Infancy, Childhood, or Adolescence." *Treatment of Psychological Disorders*, 2nd edition, 2 vols. Washington D.C.: American Psychiatric Press, 1995.

Neuwirth, S. "Reading and Learning Disorders" (pamphlet). U.S. Department of Health and Human Services, National Institute of Mental Health, 1993.

Popper, C. W., and R. J. Steingard. "Disorders Usually First Diagnosed in Infancy, Childhood, or Adolescence." *Textbook of Psychiatry*, 2nd ed. Washington D.C.: American Psychiatric Press, 1994.

Rogers, T. "Dyslexia: A Survivor's Story." *Journal of Learning Disabilities* 12, no. 2 (February 1991).

Shaffer, D., M. Campbell, et al. "Disorders Usually First Diagnosed in Infancy, Childhood, or Adolescence." *Diagnostic and Statistical Manual of Mental Disorders*, 4th edition. Washington D.C.: American Psychiatric Press, 1994.

Silver, Larry B. "Learning Disorders." Treatments of Psychiatric Disorders, 2nd edition. 2 vols. Washington D.C.: American Psychiatric Press, 1995.

Spencer, T., et al. "Comorbidity of Attention Deficit/Hyperactivity Disorder," *Review of Psychiatry* 16 (1996).

Staples, B. "Special Education Is Not a Scandal." *New York Times Magazine*, September 21, 1997.

Staub, D., and C. A. Peck. "What are the outcomes for nondisabled students?" *Educational Leadership* 52, no. 4 (April 1995).

Strub, R. L., and M. G. Wise. "Differential Diagnosis in Neuropsychiatry." *Textbook of Neuropsychiatry*, 2nd edition. 3 vols. Washington D.C.: American Psychiatric Press, 1992.

Tanner, C. Kenneth. "Inclusion in Elementary Schools: A Survey and Political Analysis." *Education Policy Analysis Archives* 3, no. 15 (October 12, 1995).

APPENDIX

GLOSSARY

Attention deficit/hyperactivity disorder (ADHD): a disorder, frequently found in conjunction with learning disorders, in which a child has trouble concentrating on tasks and may display inattention, or hyperactive or irritable behavior.

Cerebrum: the complex part of the brain that deals with more abstract processes such as reading, processing speech, and mathematics.

Disruptive behavior disorders: any of a group of disorders that cause a child to disrupt activities in home or classroom settings. Many children with learning disorders develop disruptive behaviors as a way of "acting out" their frustration. Examples are ADHD and conduct disorder.

Dyslexia/reading disorder: a disorder in which a person's ability to read words and understand them is impaired; often, letters and words seem to be transposed, or the rules that govern their arrangement seem incomprehensible.

Fetal alcohol syndrome: the name given to the effects that a child can suffer when the mother drinks alcohol while pregnant. In mild cases, fetal alcohol syndrome can cause learning disorders and other mental disorders; in more severe cases, it can cause deformities or even the death of the fetus.

Grapheme: the written symbols, such as letters or numbers, that are translated into meaning in a person's brain. Dyslexia often involves difficulty matching up graphemes with the phonemes (sounds) they represent.

Learning disorders: a group of disorders characterized by difficulty processing certain kinds of information, such as written words or mathematical symbols. Learning disorders cannot be "cured," but they can be overcome.

Mathematics disorder: a learning disorder in which a person has trouble with such acts as computation, or recognition of the symbols used in mathematics.

Mental retardation: a condition in which a person has slower or more limited than normal intellectual development or capability. Many people with learning disorders are mistakenly believed to be retarded because of their difficulties in school.

Neuroimaging: a technique that allows scientists to take pictures of brain activity to find out what parts of the brain are affected when learning disorders appear.

Phoneme: the sounds that are represented by letter combinations. Dyslexia often involves difficulty matching up phonemes with the written figures, such as letters, that represent them.

Writing disorder: a learning disorder in which a person is not able to write coherently. This often includes errors in spelling or punctuation and excessively poor handwriting. Writing disorder, or "disorder of written expression," is usually seen in conjunction with reading disorder.

APPENDIX

FURTHER READING

American Psychiatric Association. *The Diagnostic and Statistical Manual of Mental Disorders,* 4th edition. Washington, D.C.: The American Psychiatric Press, 1994.

———. *DSM-IV Sourcebook,* 3 vols. Washington, D.C.: The American Psychiatric Press, 1996.

———. *Textbook of Psychiatry,* 2nd edition. Washington, D.C.: The American Psychiatric Press, 1995.

———. *Treatment of Psychological Disorders,* 2nd edition, 2 vols. Washington, D.C.: The American Psychiatric Press, 1995.

Gazzainga, Michael S. *Mind Matters.* Boston: Houghton Mifflin, 1988.

Lyman, Donald E. *Making the Words Stand Still.* Boston: Houghton Mifflin, 1986.

McBee Knox, Jean. *Learning Disabilities.* Philadelphia: Chelsea House Publishers, 1989.

Vail, Priscilla L. *Smart Kids with School Problems.* New York: Dutton, 1987.

APPENDIX

INDEX

Orton, Samuel T., 25
Outstanding Learning Disabled
    Achievement Award, 58

Parent's Educational Resource Cen-
    ter, 74
Patton, George S., Jr., 13-15, 18-19,
    75
Phonemes, 19, 80
Phonics versus whole language, 28
Phonological processing, 56-57
Pregnancy
    complications of, 59-60
    drug use in, and learning
        disorders, 57-59
Psychiatric disorders, associated
    with learning disorders, 17

Reading aloud, 15, 75
Reading backwardness, 40
Reading disorders, 16
    causes of, 18, 60-62
    coexistence with other
        disorders, 41-42
    definitions of, 18-20
    mechanism of, 37-41
    outcomes in, 42-43
    prevalence of, 19-20
    signs of, 19
    treatment of, 73-75
    See also Dyslexia
Reading instruction methods, 28
Reading process, 37
    in brain, 56-57
    problems in, 37-41
Reading readiness skills, 60
Ritalin (methylphenidate), 34, 39, 78

Schwab, Charles, 74
Seizure disorders, 42
Self-esteem
    learning disorders and, 15, 33-

34, 42, 46, 74, 78-79
    therapy for, 71-72
Skills program, for writing disor-
    ders, 80-81
Smoking, during pregnancy, and
    learning disorders, 58-59
Social skills therapy, 73
Society, learning disorders and, 47-
    53
Socioeconomic status, low
    and diagnosis of learning
        disorders, 21
    versus learning disorders, 17
Special education, 28, 47, 50
    versus mainstreaming, 28-31,
        53
Spelling, and learning disorders, 12,
    40, 45, 80
Sports, for children with learning
    disorders, 70, 72

Teaching strategies
    for ADHD, 39
    for mathematics disorder,
        77-80
    for reading disorders, 75
    training in, 53
Tourette's syndrome, 42

Vision problems
    versus learning disorders,
        17, 62
    with reading disorders, 60-61
Whole language versus phonics, 28
Written expression disorders, 9, 16,
    46
    causes of, 62
    definition of, 22
    effects of, 45
    prevalence of, 22-23
    signs of, 22
    treatment of, 80-81

APPENDIX

PICTURE CREDITS

page

8: Ellen B. Senisi/Photo Researchers, Inc.
12: © Shirley Zeiberg Photography
14: UPI/Corbis-Bettmann
16: UPI/Corbis-Bettmann
20: Ellen B. Senisi/Photo Researchers, Inc.
24: © Shirley Zeiberg Photography
27: © Shirley Zeiberg Photography
29: photo courtesy of the Landmark School, Pride Crossing, MA
30: photo courtesy of the Landmark School, Pride Crossing, MA
32: Will & Deni McIntyre/Photo Researchers, Inc.
35: Eric R. Berndt/Unicorn Stock Photos
36: Will & Deni McIntyre/Photo Researchers, Inc.
38: Eric R. Berndt/Unicorn Stock Photos
40: Ellen B. Senisi/Photo Researchers, Inc.
46: photo courtesy of the Landmark School, Pride Crossing, MA

49: Library of Congress, #LC-USZ-62-41882
50: Ellen B. Senisi/Photo Researchers, Inc.
52: (top) UPI/Corbis-Bettmann; (bottom) Library of Congress, #LC-USZ-62-2096
54: Petit Format/Nestle/Photo Researchers, Inc.
56: Erika Stone/Photo Researchers, Inc.
61: Eric R. Berndt/Unicorn Stock Photos
64: © 1992 Terry Wild Studio
66: photo courtesy of the Landmark School, Pride Crossing, MA
68: photo courtesy of the Landmark School, Pride Crossing, MA
71: © 1997 Terry Wild Studio
72: photo courtesy of the Landmark School, Pride Crossing, MA
77: MacDonald Photography/ Unicorn Stock Photos

Senior Consulting Editor Carol C. Nadelson, M.D., is president and chief executive officer of the American Psychiatric Press, Inc., staff physician at Cambridge Hospital, and Clinical Professor of Psychiatry at Harvard Medical School. In addition to her work with the American Psychiatric Association, which she served as vice president in 1981-83 and president in 1985-86, Dr. Nadelson has been actively involved in other major psychiatric organizations, including the Group for the Advancement of Psychiatry, the American College of Psychiatrists, the Association for Academic Psychiatry, the American Association of Directors of Psychiatric Residency Training Programs, the American Psychosomatic Society, and the American College of Mental Health Administrators. In addition, she has been a consultant to the Psychiatric Education Branch of the National Institute of Mental Health and has served on the editorial boards of several journals. Doctor Nadelson has received many awards, including the Gold Medal Award for significant and ongoing contributions in the field of psychiatry, the Elizabeth Blackwell Award for contributions to the causes of women in medicine, and the Distinguished Service Award from the American College of Psychiatrists for outstanding achievements and leadership in the field of psychiatry.

Consulting Editor Claire E. Reinburg, M.A., is editorial director of the American Psychiatric Press, Inc., which publishes about 60 new books and six journals a year. She is a graduate of Georgetown University in Washington, D.C., where she earned bachelor of arts and master of arts degrees in English. She is a member of the Council of Biology Editors, the Women's National Book Association, the Society for Scholarly Publishing, and Washington Book Publishers.

As director of Write Stuff Editorial Service in New York City, **Elizabeth Russell Connelly** has written and edited for medical and business journals, trade magazines, high-tech firms, and various book publishers. She earned an MBA from New York University's Stern School in 1993 and a certificate in language studies from Freiburg Universitaet (Switzerland) in 1985. Her published work includes a global studies book for young adults; more than 14 Access travel guides covering North America, the Caribbean, and Europe; and several volumes in Chelsea House Publishers' ENCYCLOPEDIA OF PSYCHOLOGICAL DISORDERS.